D1614027

Fine Tuning Your Radial Arm Saw

# Fine Tuning Your Radial Arm Saw

by Jon Eakes

Lee Valley TOOLS LTD.

©1987, Lee Valley Tools Ltd.
ALL RIGHTS RESERVED
No part of this book may be reproduced in any form
including photocopying without permission in writing
from the publishers, except by a reviewer who may quote
brief passages in a magazine or newspaper or on radio
or television.

Lee Valley Tools Ltd.
1080 Morrison Drive
Ottawa, Ontario K2H 8K7

Distributed in the United States by:
Sterling Publishing Co., Inc.
2 Park Avenue, New York, NY 10016

Distributed in Canada by:
Sterling Publishing Co., Inc.
Georgetown Terminal Warehouses Limited
34 Armstrong Avenue
Georgetown, Ontario L7G 4R9

Photographs: Paul McCarthy
Design: Eiko Emori, MFA, MGDC, RCA

*Canadian Cataloguing in Publication Data*

ISBN 0-921335-04-0

*Printed and bound in Canada*

# Contents

# Introduction

This book is not a general manual on how to work with a radial arm saw. Nor is it a fancy list of all the gadgets you can attach to a radial with a compilation of fifty of your "favorite" projects in the appendix. It is simply a very detailed look at how to get the notoriously sloppy radial arm saw to work dead square and to a cutting tolerance of one 128th of an inch with a simple saw blade. It covers the line-up procedures and tricks that the manufacturers don't include in their owners' manuals and that the flashy text books sidestep for fear of boring you. It covers the first hour of my radial arm saw seminars that students across Canada have demanded I put down in writing.

A radial arm saw is a wonderful and versatile machine, but in talking with woodworkers across Canada, amateur and professional alike, I find that the radial is rarely used to its full potential. I can count on the fingers of one hand the number of machines I have found properly lined-up in the last several years. I constantly find salesmen, manufacturers' representatives and even school teachers who are unaware that certain adjustments exist. Store personnel who aim at the handyman seem to take the attitude that "woodworking doesn't need to be all that precise" (they love selling plastic wood and sandpaper). Manufacturers have to convince people that their machines are simple to set up and simple to use (at least simpler than those of the competition). It appears that inherent problems in the nature of a radial arm saw cannot be admitted to and dealt with by manufacturers because competitors would of course claim that their machines are problem-free. Publicity is concentrated on gadgets, not on mastering the all-important basic saw cuts.

In sum, few understand how to line the machine up and how to use it on its "precise side", and fewer still teach how this is done. As a consequence, the radial arm saw has the reputation of being an interesting but imprecise, or even dangerous, woodworking tool. With proper alignment, the radial can become the most trusted machine in your shop.

There is no one perfect machine on the market today and every woodworker will find his or her own reasons to choose one brand of machine over another. Many find important differences in the height of the tables and the accessibility of the cranks. In this book I have tried to avoid showing my own preference. More importantly, a radial arm saw is a radial arm saw whether it is made by Craftsman, DeWalt, Rockwell or someone else. The nuts and bolts are in different places and the publicity departments sing different tunes, but basically the machines are quite similar and generally have the same inherent qualities, positive and negative. When I point out a specific problem, it is not in an effort to criticize that machine but rather to face up to the shortcomings and to demonstrate how to overcome them. In this text, I have tried to show how all three of the major 10-inch radial arm saws can be kicked, coddled and cajoled into providing perfection in the cutting of wood. Other brands, models and sizes of machines can profit by the application of these same principles although you may have to find the location of the proper nuts and bolts yourself.

All photographs in the text showing various adjustments on a specific machine are brand-name identified as Craftsman, DeWalt or Rockwell. Since I wrote this book, Rockwell has changed its name to Beaver/Delta. So if you have a Beaver/Delta saw, you should follow the instructions in this book for Rockwell.

# Chapter 1

# Table Saw vs. Radial Arm Saw

The question I am most frequently asked about stationary saws is this: "Should I buy a table saw or a radial arm saw?"

The table saw is the preferred machine of almost all professional woodworkers, but this is largely due to the fact that their radials are not properly lined up and they have never received any training in the use of a radial. Hence, for the professional, the radial is usually his cut-off saw used only to shorten boards, with all his detailed work being done on the table saw.

Properly set up, the radial arm saw can be as precise and safe in cutting wood as the table saw. Both are good machines which can accomplish much of the same work. I have and use both machines, but for someone who doesn't have the money or the space for the two, let's look at the characteristics of each.

## The Table Saw

On the one hand, the table saw is a simple machine with few moving parts, hence very easy to set up and maintain. It is a stable machine which maintains its adjustments, making it excellent for production runs. Also, it can be purchased for less than a radial because it can be obtained without a motor, switch or guard.

On the other hand, the table saw requires considerable floor space, as you must be able to work all around it and have wood sticking out on all sides. Moreover, know-how, construction time and experience are required to build specialized jigs for almost all operations other than ripping. In a professional shop, most ripping is done on a band saw anyway. These jigs are usually complex because of their need to slide across the table and because of the limited adjustments of the saw blade with respect to the jig. The table saw has a theoretical advantage in precision which is usually lost in the imprecision of the jigs and their movement across the table. As well, the table saw is limited in its use of bevel angles, especially with dado or molding heads. It can also be a dangerous machine because of a hidden and often forgotten blade, especially when making dado cuts with the guard removed. Lastly, the table saw is rarely used with its guard or its splitter, as they are too much trouble to remove and replace and are rarely manufactured with any serious thought about actual use. These guards are the first victims of manufacturers' cost-cuttings.

## The Radial Arm Saw

Once correctly lined up, the radial arm saw is a simple tool to use for making simple or complex cuts. It requires few jigs and, when necessary, they are simple to make. The complications are in the machine itself. It requires little floor space as it is generally set against a wall. The left and right wings can have cupboards over them and storage space under them. The machine can be quickly changed over from one operation or adjustment to another and can cut a wide variety of miter and bevel angles with saw blades, dado heads and shaper heads. It can provide the small shop with many secondary functions which work reasonably well such as sanding, drilling and scroll sawing. In addition, it is cost-competitive if an equivalent motor, switch and guard are counted into the table saw price.

On the other hand, the radial arm saw is a complex machine to set up and to line up and requires frequent checking and minor realignment. It also needs constant cleaning of the roller head tracks and is more subject to damage or misalignment in transport than a table saw and hence less portable. It is less reliable in repeated production-run accuracy than a table saw.

Finally, it has no effective lower blade guards and can be dangerous if used improperly.

In my own shop, where I have both the radial and the table saw, I use the radial arm saw for all one-of-a-kind custom work. It is quickly moved from one adjustment to another. With the blade on the top it is easy to make eyeball cuts and minor adjustments to achieve close fits. It is quickly and accurately displaced from one rip dimension to another, whereas the table saw fence is usually out of line with the blade. I also use the radial for all cut-offs, cutting lumber to rough or finished lengths.

I use the table saw when I want to make numerous repeat cuts in production work. The number of identical cuts justifies the set-up time required to adjust the machine and its jigs. I generally cut $4' \times 8'$ panels on my table saw but this is only because I happen to have an immense table around my table saw at all times (six feet on either side of the blade and eight feet behind the blade) which makes it more than convenient to support the cut wood. With wings on either side of the radial saw and my workbench raised to the height of the saw table and placed one foot forward of the saw, I can do a reasonably equivalent job of panels on the radial.

## Recommendations

My general recommendations on the choice between the table saw and the radial saw are as follows:

a. Assuming you are willing to properly line up the radial and you are engaged primarily in one-of-a-kind production, the radial is the most efficient saw for both amateur and professional alike.

b. If you work primarily in long production runs, or only on construction sites (moving the saw around a great deal), then you will be better off with a table saw.

c. The ideal shop has one large radial for trimming lumber to length and cutting long miter cuts, one 10 inch or 12 inch radial finely tuned for custom work, one large table saw for production runs and panels, and one small table saw and an electric miter box for kicking around the back of the truck.

Obviously, for the home handyman and the small shop, I prefer the radial. But this recommendation is based upon the qualification that the machine be set up and maintained correctly to provide both precision and safety. That is what the rest of this book is all about.

# Chapter 2

# The Principles of Precision

Accurate results can only come from precise work. In this sense the "precision" of the machine and of your working techniques means the ability to work to close tolerances. Cutting wood to close tolerances at the correct dimension will result in accurately made, well-fitting joints.

Although craft books dealing with such delicate manual tasks as dovetailing and marquetry frequently deal with the details of precision, the subject is rarely discussed when dealing with power tools. Yet how can we expect to understand the importance of detailed adjustments and techniques unless we understand their role in obtaining precision from our radial arm saw? My radial and I work with six principles of precision. I will outline these principles here and then apply them in detail throughout the rest of the book.

## Snug Movement

## Positive Clamping

*"Things that move must move smoothly and firmly."*

Whenever wood and a machine come together they need to be in firm constant contact. Vibrations in the machine will mean a clattering contact between the cutting edge and the wood. A hand plane with a thin blade digs in and out of the wood grain. If the shoe of a jig saw is allowed to rise off the wood, it will not give a clean cut. Grime, dust and rough surfaces make consistent contact equally impossible.

On the radial arm saw, the biggest offender against the principle of snug movement is the roller head. It must not move freely, or even easily. Instead, it must move firmly. This is not to say that it should bind, but a loose roller head is the major cause of the "running forward" feeling with most radials. When the roller wheels are adjusted loosely on the overhead track, the entire motor assembly has a tendency to lift up during a cut, but because of the offset blade it does not lift straight up nor does it necessarily stay up. The entire motor comes rattling forward, with the saw blade climbing up on fibers it should be cutting. The cut is ragged and your right arm is quickly exhausted since you do not know if you should draw the saw forward or hold it back. When it is adjusted for "firm" travel you rarely have this problem. You must, however, clean the track several times a day (exactly 23 seconds of work) since the least bit of dust or accumulated grime will block its movement and make drawing it forward firm but jerky. What we want is firm, smooth movement.

The column must move up and down smoothly and firmly in the base casting. Too much freedom here can cause the arm to pivot upward or sideways or both. Too tight and it binds and becomes jerky.

Similarly, the arm-to-column connection must be firm and free from slack.

It is equally important that when the wood moves, it too moves firmly and smoothly. This is why I include hold-downs as part of the fine tuning of a radial arm saw.

*"Things that should not move, must not move."*

Almost all adjustments on woodworking machines hold their positions by means of friction clamps; two surfaces that bind together relatively solidly by pressure alone. Hand planes as well as power planers hold their blades by friction. Table saw depth adjustments are locked by friction. The radial arm saw relies on friction all over.

Whereas bolts and pins lock things absolutely into position, friction clamps hold them "positively". This means that they should clamp sufficiently solidly to prevent the pressures that the saw will exert on them from moving their position. At the same time however, they should not be over-tightened to either harm the machine or tire your hands.

The prime example is the arm-to-column clamp (the miter clamp). If the arm is set at 30° on the miter scale and the clamp is engaged, it will always be possible to force the arm to 35° despite the clamp because of the tremendous leverage you have on the end of the arm. Trying to tighten it so that it would be impossible to move would rapidly wear the cam parts or break a pivot somewhere along the linkage. It must be set tightly enough to effectively resist the lateral forces of the cutting action of the saw. These forces are actually rather minor except when ripping. This exception can be dealt with by proper use of the fixed 90° indexing as will be explained in the alignment procedure.

People tend to tighten the bevel clamp so tightly that the handle eventually breaks and gets replaced by a pair of vice-grips. The common cause of this is failure to appreciate that the 90° index point can be calibrated

## Use of the End Point of Slack

to be dead on. As a result, some people keep trying to set the bevel to 1° or 2° in an effort to get a square cut. But at 1° it clamps very poorly (the beveled indexing pin itself is fighting the setting) and overkill becomes the standard procedure.

The use of sandpaper in certain circumstances can help to achieve positive clamping without undue pressure. This is explained when we consider the sandpaper miter fence and wooden feather boards.

Surprisingly enough, even chipping on the bottom side of the cut can be eliminated. It's a question of clean back-up and eliminating vibration between the wood and the table (as with my "fence hold-down" jig).

*"Slack always has an end point – let's use it."*

Ignoring slack in screw drives and indexing pins leads to sloppy results. You must take up the slack right to its end point to maintain precision.

The arm-to-column indexing pin must have some slack in its adjustment or the pin simply will not pivot in and out of its indexing slots. This means that when the pin is indexed to 90°, the saw may very well be cutting at 88° or 91°. In fact, many people find it hard to get the same result twice. If, however, either end point of slack is defined and calibrated to exactly 90°, then the saw could be set to exactly 90° every time despite the slack. I seat the pin into the column and, before clamping it tight, shove the arm to the right until it comes to a full stop against the indexed pin. It is this "end point of slack" that I calibrate to exactly 90° and it stays there, waiting, dead-on every time.

When a screw drive is used in any machine, there is always slack between the screw threads and the nut threads. Although the threads may be an exact dimension (such as 1/8″ per revolution), changing the direction of rotation will throw the slack into any effort to use screw pitch for depth measurements. If turning is done only in one direction, you will be sitting firmly on the end point of slack all the way and depth adjustments can easily be made to one 128th of an inch (if the column is sliding smoothly and firmly) by simply watching the crank handle position. With the blade in the horizontal position, this allows for cutting surprisingly accurate box joints without either measuring or marking the wood.

Principle 4

## Squaring to Actual Work Surfaces

*"Align a machine at its production end."*

Too often, instructions tell us to square the saw up to the table rails or some other reference point that is not the same surface that will be holding the wood. Even lining up the table and then attaching a covering can change the angle of the cut in the wood. It is the final table surface and the final fence which should serve as reference points for alignment of the saw.

If temporary tables or fence additions are added, the actual angle of cut in the wood should be verified before trying to produce accurate results, since the precision of your machine may have been compromised by inaccuracies in your temporary additions or their installation.

Principle 5

## Verification on Cut Wood

*"Rough static alignment is done with instruments on the machine; dynamic fine tuning is done with a blade cutting wood."*

It doesn't matter if a jointer, for example, looks good. What counts is whether or not it produces straight square boards. This is always the final test of alignment.

There are two reasons for using wood cuts, not metal squares, as the fine tuning instruments for a radial arm saw.

Firstly, by using manipulation tricks when cutting wood, you can adjust the saw square to the table for a 6″ depth and square from the fence for a 26″ cut – twice the actual cutting capacity of the machine. This means that within its actual cutting capacities, it will be twice as precise as can possibly be measured with metal squares.

Secondly, the end product is really what counts. Hence, I don't care if something may look out of line on the machine as long as the blade passing through wood gives me the perfection I demand. This difference in apparent alignment and actual cutting results can be due to the fact that the metal square by necessity gives a static picture of the machine's alignment. The blade engaged in wood gives a dynamic measurement identical to actual working conditions.

# Definition of Entry Before Cutting

*"Know where the blade will cut before cutting."*

We often scratch up the edge of a piece of wood or create considerable scrap trying to determine exactly where the point of entry will be for a cutting edge. Whether with drill press or table saw, we are used to a lot of trial and error.

The fence on a radial arm saw is usually a sorry looking chopped-up mess, often hiding down below the wood to be cut. The gaping hole in the vicinity of where the blade passes through the table provides no back-up against splinters on the back side of the cut and certainly is useless in guessing where the blade will strike the workpiece.

You must get used to the idea that the fence can be shifted an inch or two to the right or the left without really affecting its function at all as a back stop. This shifting allows you to put the fence in its normal position during line-up and general work, and then, when you want to get down to the business of precision, slide it over to a clean spot and make a nice fresh through-cut. This new cut defines quite precisely both sides of the kerf you are about to make and protects against splintering on the backside of the workpiece at the same time. If, in addition, the fence is about 1/4″ higher than the wood you are to cut, this slot in the fence becomes a precise index against which cut marks on the workpiece can be accurately placed before ever coming near them with the blade. See Fig. 2-1.

Fig 2-1 *The fence as an alignment tool for cross cutting*

Unfortunately there is no precision guide for ripping, so the final check on a rip setting is actually to cut a piece of wood and verify the results before putting the real workpiece to the blade.

# Chapter 3

# Adjusting the Radial Arm Saw

In general terms, I begin my adjustments by stabilizing the machine, then snugging up all moving and clamping tensions. Next, I prepare the table plane as the base of all squaring adjustments, following which I work on squaring all the cuts and finally breaking in the table. Actually, this sequence is applicable to any woodworking machine, but most people leave stabilization and adjusting tensions as an afterthought – a fatal error.

Aligning a radial arm saw reminds me of building pyramids – if you don't put the bottom down first and the top on last, it won't stand up for very long (if at all). Although there is some room for variation in the order of adjustments, I recommend following my sequence to assure adjustments (that can alter subsequent adjustments) are done in the proper consecutive order.

The first full workout you give your machine could take three or four hours; most of that time being spent in reading this book, studying the photos and trying to find the screws on your machine. After years of experience preparing for seminars, it usually takes me twenty minutes to line up a new machine. Once you have brought your machine into precision alignment the first time, a weekly tune-up can be done in five minutes going through all the same steps but stopping to adjust only where things are out of line. Things being out of line are usually caused by abusive use or transport, or by honest wearing of any of the moving parts, particularly the column keyway screws. Although I check my shop machine constantly, I actually make adjustments quite rarely.

## Stabilizing the Stand

## Assembling and Covering the Table

Although the radial arm saw can function in a free-standing position, you will find that it is easier to use if it is fixed solidly. Either screw the feet to the floor or run $1'' \times 4''$ stabilizers from the frame back to a solid attachment on the wall. If you do nothing else, at least ensure that the feet are leveled up to eliminate any wobble.

I have seen recommendations to set the saw on a slight backward tilt; the reasoning being that the roller head will roll back to its neutral position all by itself. For God's sake, if your roller head is loose enough to roll anywhere by itself, unplug the saw quickly – you have a dangerous machine! The roller head should be snug enough that it won't go anywhere unless you put it there (see Procedure 5 on sliding tensions). Your saw should be relatively level, but exact levelling to the ground with a carpenter's level is unnecessary. What must be exact is the relationship between the table and the arm – not necessarily the table and the ground (refer to Procedure 6).

Completely assemble the table, without bothering to try lining it up to the saw. Precision adjustment of the table rails at this time is useless as they can get knocked out when you cover the table. In fact you're not ready to line anything up at all until you finish Tension Procedures 4 and 5. Follow the manufacturer's instructions in the table assembly, skipping over any line-up efforts at this point.

If you are installing a new table top not supplied by the manufacturer with pre-drilled mounting holes, then you must take care that the rails are mounted in symmetrical fashion, each one being the same distance back from the front edge of the table. The best bet is to copy the size and layout of the original table. If you want to make the table oversize or add extensions, see "Table Extensions" in Chapter 6 to avoid potential problems. The best, most stable table tops are made from $3/4''$ or even $1''$ high-density composition board. Excellent table tops can also be made from $3/4''$ 9-layer hardwood plywood, although it can be costly and hard to find.

Fig 3-1 *Table cover*

Now we want to cover the table "base" with a disposable working surface. This way the table base never needs to be changed again. Fig. 3-1 shows a $1/4''$ plywood cover placed over the front portion of the table. Quality finished plywood rather than shop-grade plywood is best for this application. Both sides should be smooth and free from defects to fit properly to the table base and to provide a smooth working surface. Masonite is not recommended here because it is unnecessarily hard on saw blades and moves too much with moisture changes. The cover should fit both sides and the front of the table exactly. It should fall $1/16''$ to $1/8''$ short of the fence as seen in the photograph. This is an important little detail since without the small gap, slivers of wood are constantly catching between the fence and table – holding the workpiece away from the fence in an untrue fashion. It is bothersome and often difficult to remove these slivers, sometimes requiring loosening of the fence. The small gap between the table cover and the fence eliminates all of that. Splinters which collect there can be blown or brushed away easily whenever necessary as they don't jam into the crack.

No effort is made to cover the back side of the table, or even the $1^{1}/2''$ spacer. There are two reasons for this. First of all, with the back table $1/4''$ lower than the front table, we can drop the blade $1/8''$ into the table cover for an ordinary cut, but it still floats above the back table to allow swinging into miter positions without having to lift the blade. When the fence is moved back to either rear position, we are almost always ripping quite far forward on the front table. Hence our workpiece is well supported near the blade. The fact that the back portion of the table is $1/4''$ lower will rarely affect the cut. If it is a problem in a special case, a $1/4''$ filler can be set in for that job.

I attach the table cover with small brass tacks (brass so that if they are struck by the blade there is no damage and no spark) together with a conservative blob of rubber cement (obtainable at stationery stores) at the location of each tack and all along the rear line of the table cover. Do not use contact cement as it is too strong. The glue is there to assure that the cover stays down and flat and that no sawdust sneaks under it at the fence, but leaving it relatively easy to pry up and change when it gets too chewed up. The tacks are there to hold the cover down tight while the glue dries. If you have other means of pressing the two pieces together you can skip the tacks completely. See Fig. 3-2 for an idea of the placement of the tacks so that they avoid the primary zones of saw cutting. Make sure to countersink the tacks just below the surface of the cover.

25

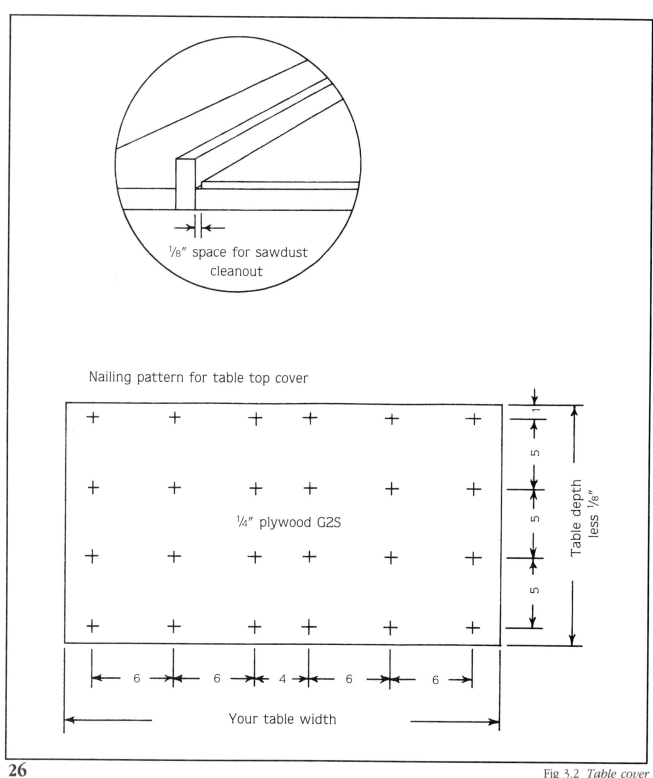

⅛″ space for sawdust
cleanout

Nailing pattern for table top cover

¼″ plywood G2S

Table depth less ⅛″

1

5

5

5

6   6   4   6   6

Your table width

Fig 3.2 *Table cover*

# Cleaning Your Saw

Taking the initiative to pull off and replace this table cover when the old one gets rather sloppy can make a very big difference in the precision of your work. In Procedure 14 of the adjustments, we will talk about kerf cutting into this table cover. During the normal operation of your saw, take care to avoid continually dropping the blade a bit lower as you will quickly cut through the $1/4''$ top. It will then require immediate replacement as sawdust will slide under and create a bulge in the middle of the table.

Radial arm saws need more cleaning than lubricating. They need cleaning when they are new out of the box as well as daily and regular cleaning.

If you have a new machine, start by filing off sharp corners that are sure to rap your knuckles. The DeWalt is the worst offender, with knife-sharp corners on the motor nameplate sitting right next to the guard nut. A quick touch with a small smooth file and the nameplate becomes inoffensive. The column base near the table screws needs filing on the Craftsman and the yoke casting near the bevel clamp needs rounding off on the Rockwell (of course as soon as the manufacturers read this book, the new models will no longer have these problems!).

The whole machine should be kept dusted clean, and all moving parts should be kept polished clean. Dust and chips on the table and against the fence can change the angles between the wood and the blade. Wood dust allowed to fall between the fence and the table before tightening it into place will put the machine out of square.

Keeping moving parts polished clean is the only way we can properly adjust the sliding tensions in Procedure 5 and obtain the precision I claim for the radial arm saw. Cleaning the back column is a regular task and cleaning the motor roller track and bearings is a daily task which under certain dusty conditions may have to be done several times a day. It is quite quick and easy and the difference in operation justifies the little trouble.

WD-40 is the standard cleaning material recommended by most people. It does clean and tends to leave a slight lubricating film. The problem with it is that, despite claims to the contrary, it collects grime deposits more rapidly than when the machine is cleaned with a pure cleaner like ammonia. See Fig. 3-3. I find a good balance by using WD-40 about every third cleaning and ammonia the rest of the time. This is cheaper and puts the accent on cleaning, not lubricating. By the way, when you clean don't be too cheap. Clean with a clean rag. Otherwise you may put on more grime than you take off.

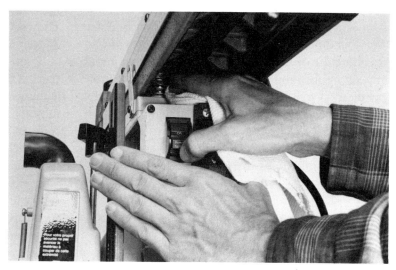

Fig 3-4 *Cleaning rollers*

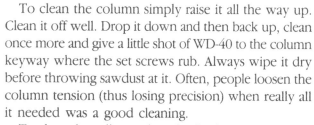

Fig 3-3 *Cleaners*

To clean the column simply raise it all the way up. Clean it off well. Drop it down and then back up, clean once more and give a little shot of WD-40 to the column keyway where the set screws rub. Always wipe it dry before throwing sawdust at it. Often, people loosen the column tension (thus losing precision) when really all it needed was a good cleaning.

To clean the roller track and roller bearings, start by pushing the machine all the way back. Apply cleaner to the rag or the track and wipe all the exposed track. Be careful with the DeWalt and the Rockwell as they have machined tracks which usually have sharp edges. You can cut your fingers if they are not well covered by the rag. Then push the machine forward and clean the rear portion of the track.

Now clean the roller bearings that ride in or on the tracks. Fig. 3-4 shows the technique on the DeWalt. It is the same for the Rockwell and similar for the Craftsman except that the latter has its roller bearings on the outside and is slightly more difficult to reach because of the protective coverings. Pull the motor forward. Apply cleaner to the rag. Push the rag up against the roller and push away from your rag. The roller will turn against the rag and clean itself. Do not pull the motor toward the rag or you will pinch your finger between the roller and the track. The back rollers are cleaned by getting behind the motor, applying the rag and pushing toward the front of the arm – always away from your finger so as not to pinch it in the track.

After the rollers are cleaned, wipe the track once more to pick up deposits made while cleaning the rollers.

The whole procedure takes about 23 seconds but the results make you realize clearly that you are working with a precision machine, not a clunky circular saw hung on a rail. The difference is as clear as comparing a keen chisel edge to a dull one.

## Adjusting the Clamps

## The Arm-to-Column Clamp Adjustment

Here, we are going to put into practice the principle of positive clamping – "things that should not move, must not move." As I stated previously, our guideline is that clamps should clamp solidly enough to prevent the pressures that the saw will exert on them from moving their position, but at the same time not be over tightened to either harm the machine or tire your hands.

Fig 3-5 *Testing arm-to-column clamp*

Fig. 3-5 shows the procedure for testing the adjustment of the arm-to-column clamp. The arm is swung to any position between 0° and 45°, i.e., the indexing pin will not lock into the column. Then the clamp is fully applied. Now grasp the table with one hand and place the other hand on the end of the arm. Apply pressure to the end of the arm as if to bring it back to the 0° position. The only thing resisting movement of the arm is the arm-to-column clamp. It is always possible to "force" the arm to move because of the tremendous leverage the long arm gives. What we are looking for is a reasonable holding power so that it won't move easily. The direction of force while sawing in a miter position is generally back towards the column, not sideways against the arm, so the saw will never apply as much pressure against this clamp as you are now applying during this test (Procedure 10 will take care of the exceptional case of pressure during ripping operations). If the arm moves too easily you will need to tighten the clamp adjustment. If it is impossible or difficult to lock the clamp, then you will need to loosen the clamp adjustment. How hard should it be to lock the clamp? When testing, it should be as loose as possible while still resisting firm pressure on the end of the arm.

## Craftsman

Fig 3-6

The locking cam on the Craftsman is adjusted by way of a finger knob accessible from under the arm as shown in Fig. 3-6. Simply release the clamp, turn the knob slightly with your finger, and then test it again.

## DeWalt

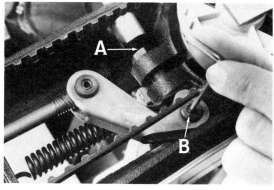

Fig 3-7

To adjust the DeWalt you must remove the cover on the arm (they call it a shroud). Fig. 3-7 indicates the adjustment bolt at point A. This can best be reached with a socket wrench, although you can manage to get an open-ended wrench to work from above. Point B in the photo indicates the locking set screw that must be released before adjusting A and then retightened after the adjustment. As in all the DeWalt locking set screws, there is a little brass plug between the set screw and the adjusting bolt. Don't lose it as it prevents damage to the threads of the adjusting bolt.

After some wear or serious adjustment, the clamp control handle located in the front end of the arm may not travel fully in the open or the clamped positions without striking the housing casting. If this is the case, the locking set screw shown in Fig. 3-8 must be loosened and the link shaft turned in or out to properly position the handle for both operations. Retighten the locking set screw.

## Rockwell

Fig 3-9

The Rockwell arm-to-column clamp is self-adjusting in the sense that it has a screw action and not a cam action like the others. Fig. 3-9 shows its position. You should use the same test procedure outlined above to learn how hard you should tighten this screw. People tend to over-tighten it for fear of something moving. You need it tight enough to pass the test but not so tight as to wear parts before their time nor tire your hands.

## The Yoke Clamp Adjustment

Fig 3-10 *Testing the yoke clamp*

Fig. 3-10 shows the procedure for testing the yoke clamp adjustment. Disengage the yoke indexing pin and swing the motor halfway around between a cross cut and a rip cut so that the indexing pin is not engaged. Lock the yoke clamp firmly. Now grasp the motor with both hands and try to swing it back into the cross cut position. It should not move at all.

If the motor does move, the yoke handle needs adjusting. It may also need adjusting if it hits the yoke casting in either the release or the clamp position.

**DeWalt**

Fig 3-8

## Craftsman

Fig 3-11

To adjust the yoke clamp on the Craftsman, it is necessary to remove the carriage from the arm. This is done by removing the arm cap in the front of the arm and also removing the Allen-head bolt which acts as a carriage stop. Whenever removing the carriage from the arm, be careful to pull it straight forward and all the way off so as not to force the back roller bearings. Hold it very straight when going back onto the arm until all four rollers are safely onto their rails.

Put the yoke clamp handle in the unlocked position and tighten the central nut as shown in Fig. 3-11. The handle should now lock when approximately halfway between the two sides of the yoke.

## DeWalt

Fig 3-12

Fig. 3-12 shows the butterfly lock that adjusts the yoke clamp on the DeWalt. Ideally, the clamp will be locked when the clamp handle is about halfway between the two sides of the yoke. To adjust, use a screwdriver to bend one of the butterfly wings down over the stop lug and then rotate the entire butterfly – counter-clockwise to tighten; clockwise to loosen. Make sure that the stop lug is located in a locking position between the two wings of the butterfly. If for some reason this adjustment doesn't want to work, you will have to remove the carriage from the arm and tighten the king nut in the same manner as explained above for the Craftsman.

## Rockwell

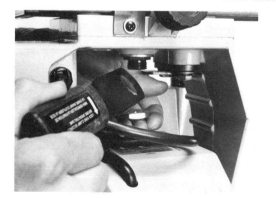

Fig 3-13

If the yoke clamp handle will not lock before striking the yoke casting on the Rockwell, you must remove the handle and reposition it on its mounting. Fig. 3-13 shows the one nut that must be removed. The handle drops off and is simply repositioned one flat on the shaft and the nut is then replaced.

# The Bevel Clamp Adjustment

## Craftsman

Replace the carriage on the arm. Don't forget to replace the bolt that acts as a carriage stop in the end of the arm. Now repeat the test shown in Fig. 3-10.

The bevel clamp is tested in the same manner as the other clamps as shown in Fig. 3-14. Set the bevel angle to about 30° to ensure that the indexing pin is not engaged and then lock the clamp. With both hands, try to force the motor out of its position. If it moves, you need to tighten the clamp adjustment. If it is extremely difficult to close the bevel clamping handle, it has been over-tightened. Handles are often broken off by people over-tightening them – usually resorting to hammers and vise-grips for leverage. I have found two common causes for this over-tightening error.

Fig 3-14 *Testing bevel clamp*

If oil or some other lubricant gets between the two friction plates or rings clamped by this handle, it will not hold. Clamping surfaces are one area of the radial that should not be cleaned with WD-40 at all; only with ammonia or solvent.

The second common cause of over-tightening is that the blade is not lined up to a proper 90° to the table but rather 1°–2° off. When you try to set the bevel angle that close to an indexing point for more than an occasional cut, the indexing pin itself will tend to shove the bevel over to its indexing point. If you compensate by tightening the clamp rather than by adjusting the indexing pin to a proper 90°, you are generally obliged to over-tighten the handle and force something to the breaking point.

33

## Craftsman

Fig 3-15

The Craftsman is adjusted by removing the clamp handle and repositioning it on the clamping bolt. Fig. 3-15 shows the removal of the holding screw in order to drop the handle down. This can be done without removing the handle and the bevel scale (they were removed in the photograph to show the mechanism more clearly). Be careful here because the clamping bolt has a left-handed thread. If you accidentally unscrew it from its nut, you will have to remove the saw handle and the bevel scale as in the photo in order to put the nut back onto the bolt. Once the clamp handle has been positioned (using the above test to properly clamp the bevel position), screw the holding screw firmly back into position.

## DeWalt

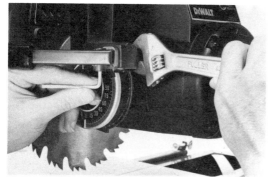

Fig 3-16

The DeWalt uses a cam action to clamp the bevel. Fig. 3-16 shows the use of a small hex wrench to release the locking set screw to permit adjustment of the locking bolt. Here you must be especially careful because if you remove this set screw, a small brass plug, which protects the bolt threads from the set screw, will fall out and get lost. Tighten the bolt from the back as in the photo. After testing the clamp, don't forget to tighten the locking set screw.

## Rockwell

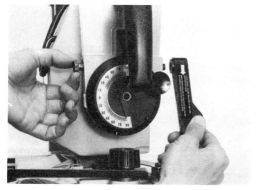

Fig 3-17

To adjust the bevel clamp handle on the Rockwell, the motor must be placed in a vertical position as in Fig. 3-17. Then the handle can be swung counter-clockwise until it comes right off the clamping bolt. The bolt should be pulled carefully out of its socket on the left side, rotated one flat of the hex head and pushed back into its socket. The handle is then screwed back onto the other end and the tension tested.

34

## The Rip Clamp Adjustment

## Fence Clamps

The rip clamp simply prevents the carriage from moving on the arm during rip operations. As shown in Fig. 3-18, the test to see if it is working effectively is simply to tighten the knob, then try pushing the carriage. All three machines work in the same fashion.

Fig 3-18 *Testing rip clamp*

If it does not clamp, the cause is usually not an adjustment but a missing part, as some of the clamps have a brass insert which presses against the arm casting. If it is missing, the screw will not reach the arm. If it is not missing, this part takes many years to wear out.

One problem which arises occasionally is that the clamp slowly closes because of motor vibrations during cross-cutting, causing an annoying drag or blockage in the travel of the carriage. This problem is easily eliminated by removing the clamping knob and giving the bolt threads one good squeeze with a pair of vice-grips. This will give the bolt just enough resistance to movement so that it won't move by itself.

In all three machines the fence is clamped into place by finger screws driven from the back of the rear table. Make sure that these screws have the protective washers on the leading edges to protect the table and to give better pressure. Do not tighten them too much – you'll only wear your fingers out. The greatest problem here is sawdust or chips being allowed to get between the fence and the table before clamping. This can bend the fence or throw it out of square with respect to the travel of the blade. Wipe it clean every time the fence is moved or changed.

Craftsman's dust collector and most homemade dust collectors fail to give enough access and clearance to these screws to allow them to be used easily without having to remove the dust collector. Therefore, plan room into your designs.

Years ago, DeWalt had a great cam system operated from up front under the main table. This eliminated that far reach to the back. It was, of course, a victim of cost cutting. For the inventive woodworker this could be a useful modification to your machine.

Procedure 5

# Adjusting Sliding Tensions

Here we are going to put into practice the principle of snug movement – "things that move must move smoothly and firmly".

Woodworkers are often proud of some of their fine tools and machines, showing off the way in which the parts fit together like a Swiss clock. Yet these same people will all too often accept the fact that their radial arm saws rattle along in the corner as sloppy as can be. This "rattling" looseness has a series of important consequences.

First of all, many machines – like the radial arm saw – can become dangerous. A rattling loose roller head will tend to jump up and down and charge forward as it tries to climb up on the wood. Secondly, all hope of precision will be lost as the blade changes its bevel angles from instant to instant, the arm swings right and left and the column leans forward and backward. Thirdly, your work is ragged and full of surface splinters as the saw chops through the bottom and the heel fails to follow the toe. Perhaps the most unfortunate result of failure to properly adjust the sliding tensions of radial arm saws is that the saws get a bad reputation. If you put together a sports car as loosely as most people assemble their saws, you could never hope to stay on the road.

*Snug* is about as hard a word to define in a book as *taste*. How loose is "rattling", how tight is "binding" and just when have we found "snug"? If you were to drive a new Mercedes and then a very old Ford, you would easily feel what I mean by the word "snug". Yes, your crummy old radial arm saw can be tuned up to run like a new Mercedes. Keep reading.

On each of the adjustments, I have tried to give you a specific test procedure which will help to answer this question. Generally speaking, a "snug sliding tension" is one that requires a "firm" action on your part to move it but has no tendency to move in increments. The roller head moves smoothly and the column does not drop down in jumps. A "snug" tension requires frequent cleaning of the two surfaces, and in fact a sliding action that appears to be binding may be found to be too loose once you clean out all the grime that has been deposited between the moving parts.

# Roller Head to Arm

The way in which the whole motor carriage rides in the arm track is the most important of the sliding tension adjustments. I have rarely found a machine with a properly tensioned roller head. When this is loose it not only moves up and down, but because of the fact that the blade is off-set to one side, the bevel angle will change as it rattles along.

The weight of the motor tends to hide slop here. Put your hand under the motor and lift. Is there a clicking sound in the track? That is, are the rollers so loose that they can move up and down in or on the track? Well, that's exactly what happens every time you try to cut a piece of wood. However, the saw is so noisy that you don't hear it. Our objective here is to ensure that the carriage rollers are in firm contact with both the top and the bottom of their tracks for the full length of their travel – without making them so tight as to force or wear the tracks.

Before performing the following test, make sure that you have cleaned the tracks and the carriage rollers.

Fig 3-19 *Testing roller tension*

Place your thumb directly on the carriage roller wheel as shown in Fig. 3-19. Press hard and with your other hand push the carriage away from your thumb (pulling towards your thumb will seriously pinch your skin). If you are able to stop the wheel from rolling, it is too loose. Making this test while wearing a rubber glove is easier on your thumb and really ensures that the roller is not slipping.

You must also repeat this test on one of the rear wheels, remembering to push the carriage away from your thumb (toward the front of the arm).

If the wheels are too loose, you will have to tighten them as shown in the following sections. If the carriage is binding and you believe it to be too tight, follow the adjustment instructions but loosen rather than tighten the sliding tension, then re-test to be sure you have not made them too loose. It should move smoothly, but you should not be able to stop the wheel while moving the carriage.

## Craftsman

Fig 3-20

On the Craftsman, the adjustable rollers are on the left hand side of the carriage. You will have to remove the side cover to get at them. See Fig. 3-20.

The wrench in the picture is about to be placed on the eccentric bolt of the rear roller. First you must slightly loosen the locking nut that is on that bolt. It can be found under the mounting assembly. Then you turn the eccentric bolt a bit to the right or left, hold it in place and tighten the nut below. Test for the proper tension and then perform the same adjustment procedure for the second roller.

Tightening the locking nut tends to move the bolt a slight amount, changing your adjustment. Hold the upper wrench very solidly, or move it a little too far so that when the lock nut shifts it a bit, it ends up in the proper position (that's not really cheating, just bending with the wind rather than fighting it).

The Craftsman carriage rollers ride on steel rods attached to the sides of the arm casting. When adjusted to be snug, you may find that the carriage moves unevenly across the

## DeWalt

Fig 3-21

The two rollers on the left of the machine are adjustable in the DeWalt. There is a locking nut just ahead of the wrench in Fig. 3-21 and the bottom of the roller shaft can be reached with an Allen key from underneath. Allen keys with two long legs, like those provided with new saws, work best for both reach and leverage. In order to expose the adjustable shafts from underneath, you must put the saw in the "out-rip" position, that is, the handle to the right.

Loosen the locking nut, turn the eccentric shaft left or right with the Allen key, and retighten the locking nut.

Always retighten before testing, since the act of retightening can change the adjustment a little bit. This tendency of locking nuts to move an adjustment can be compensated

## Rockwell

Fig 3-22

The adjustable rollers on the Rockwell are the two on the left hand side of the carriage (the photo of Fig. 3-22 was taken from the back of the machine). To get to them you must remove the cover over the top of the arm.

As on the other machines, the shafts of the adjustable rollers are eccentric shafts, locked into place with a locking nut. You will find what looks like two nuts, one on top of the other. The small one on the top is the locking nut and must be slightly loosened to make any adjustments. Then the larger nut is moved to the right or left to move the roller into or away from the track. Retighten the locking nut before testing the sliding tension again.

# Arm-to-Column: Vertical Pivot

### Craftsman

full length of the arm. This can be due to uneven wear on these rods, but more frequently it is because sawdust has managed to get behind the rods and push them forward in between their mounting screws. You may have to remove the rods and clean behind them. I have seen their performance improved by adding two additional mounting screws to hold them tighter to the arm. Also, with great care not to gum up the wheels, you could seal up the crack between the rod and the arm where the dust gets in. Athough these "rod tracks" wear faster than the "machined tracks" on the other two machines, they have the theoretical advantage of being replaceable. I say theoretical because I've seen 30 year old machines on which the machined tracks are still in good shape.

### DeWalt

for by placing the eccentric shaft out of adjustment a little bit in the opposite direction from that which the locking nut will take when tightened. The shift caused by tightening the locking nut will then leave the shaft in its correct position (it's precise results we want, no matter how we get there).

Test the wheel again for snugness. When it is correct, repeat the same procedure for the other adjustable wheel.

### Rockwell

As with all these kinds of locking nut arrangements, tightening the locking nut has a tendency to rotate the adjustment shaft a little, changing the adjustment. Be careful to hold the adjusting nut firmly while tightening the locking nut. You can also "overcompensate" the position of the adjusting nut so that when the locking nut moves the shaft a bit, it ends up in the correct position. It is the result that counts, not how we get there.

The arm should be snugly attached to the column, although it must be just loose enough to allow swinging the arm from side to side for miter cuts. Slop in this adjustment is rarely recognized because the weight of both the arm and the motor pull the arm down to one side of any vertical play. However, a loose connection between the arm and the column can cause uneven depth of cut when making dados as well as increasing the tendency of the saw to run forward.

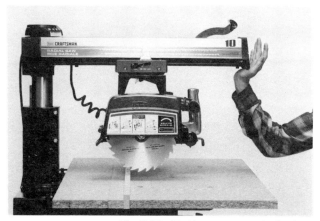

Fig 3-23 *Testing arm vertical pivot*

To test your machine, first release the arm-to-column clamp. Then place your hand as shown in Fig. 3-23 and lift up. If there is definite travel and then a stop (not just a bit of flex), you need to tighten the adjustment. You must not, however, tighten it so tight that with the arm-to-column clamp released it is difficult to swing the arm left and right to position it for miter cuts.

## Craftsman

Fig 3-24

To adjust the arm-to-column vertical play on the Craftsman, you must remove the cover on the rear of the arm as shown in Fig. 3-24. There are four bolts that harness the arm to the column. The two upper bolts are the primary adjustment bolts. Adjust them to remove the play as explained in the test section. Then snug up to the two lower bolts but not as tightly as the upper ones. The photo shows the wrench on one of the lower bolts.

## DeWalt

Fig 3-25

that comes with the saw. If the nut is backed off to the left it can be used to force the casting open. If it is simply loosened and the Allen key is used to tighten the bolt; the casting will then squeeze in on the column. The lock nut should then be locked into place to the right.

If slight adjustment here does not eliminate vertical play properly, then the arm cover must be removed to expose an identical bolt and locking nut about two inches higher up. They should be adjusted to the same tension top and bottom.

The tension on the fit of the arm to the column on the DeWalt is controlled by two bolts which force open or closed the split casting of the arm itself. Fig. 3-25 shows the location of one of these bolts. The locking nut is in the crack and best reached with the small end of the thin-blade wrench

## Rockwell

Fig 3-26

There is no adjustment on the Rockwell for the sliding tension of the arm-to-column attachment. A simple pin runs through the top of the column to prevent the arm from lifting off. See Fig. 3-26.

Despite the absence of adjustment here, I must say that the machines I have checked were finely enough machined that there was no arm-to-column play and, given the infrequence of movement of this joint, it is not likely that much play would wear into this joint in the foreseeable future.

# Column-to-Base: Rise, Fall and Pivot

The column rise, fall and pivot (or vertical play) constitute three different test procedures but only one adjustment for all three sliding tensions. The objective here is to ensure that the column moves properly without permitting it to introduce any error into the saw cutting.

The adjustments described in this section could be affected by the column key adjustments made to prevent column-to-base rotation described in the next section. Look at that section to see how to back off the column key adjustments so that they will not affect the rise, fall and pivot tests. That will leave the arm swinging freely a couple of inches to the right and left, but don't let that worry you for the moment. Clamp the arm-to-column clamp (miter clamp) down tight to eliminate all movement between the arm and the column.

If you haven't done so already, thoroughly clean off the column as described in Procedure 3. A dirty column works quite differently from a clean one.

Fig 3-27 *Testing column pivot*

As shown in Fig. 3-27, lift the end of the arm while watching the column/base joint. If you can see pivoting, or feel anything more than simple flex of the casting, you will find that one of your adjustment screws is much too loose. It could be that everything is terribly loose back there or that the top or bottom of the base casting is holding the column while the other end allows for a great deal of movement.

Fig 3-28 *Testing column rise*

Testing for smooth rise is simple. Pull the motor out to the front end of the arm to put a stress on the base casting. Crank the arm up to the top. It should move smoothly, perhaps requiring a little more effort than you are used to, but not demanding that you force the crank handle. If it moves up in jumps, clean the column. If it still moves up in jumps, the base is too tight around the column.

You will notice that it is always easier to crank the column up with the motor all the way at the back. This is where it should be placed when you wish to crank up during normal operation of the machine.

Fig 3-29 *Testing column fall*

With the motor still on the end of the arm as shown in Fig. 3-29, slowly crank the column down. You will find one of three conditions.

If the saw rattles and vibrates all the way down, the base is too loose around the column. It is banging from side to side as it comes down.

If the saw drops in jerks, the base is too tight around the column. In fact, it has a friction fit to the column which holds it up in the air while the drive screw takes up the slack in its screw drive, pushes against the control nut and finally forces the column downward. It then falls to the other end of the slack in the drive screw,

freezes tight again until the screw picks up the slack and forces it to jump down again. The column must be loosened up.

If the column will come down without either vibrating or jumping, the sliding tension in the base is just right. This is what we are looking for: the middle ground between the two.

Each of the three different machines has two adjusting bolts in the base to control sliding tension with the column. Although this is necessary to obtain a very good fit over such a distance, it complicates the adjustment because often we don't know which one is too tight or too loose.

Although I have no absolute fixed procedure for playing with these two bolts to obtain the proper sliding tension, I recommend the following sequence. Loosen the lower bolt. Tighten or loosen the upper bolt at the same time that you are cranking the column downward (if you can reach that far) until it falls between loose vibrations and tight jerking. Then tighten the lower bolt just until it begins to interfere with the travel of the column. You may have to return and loosen the upper one a bit when the lower one pulls the castings in. Tighten the locking nuts and run all three tests again. If you are just a bit too loose, stop. The column key adjustment of the next section will make up the difference.

## Craftsman

Fig 3-30

As you can see in Fig. 3-30, Craftsman provides two brightly plated bolts in the base so that you will have no trouble identifying the adjusting bolts. There are no locking nuts on these bolts. They hold on the principle of spring tension from the castings themselves. Tightening or loosening these bolts will tighten and loosen the sliding tension between the base and the column.

## DeWalt

Fig 3-31

The DeWalt has the two adjustment bolts spread well apart. In Fig. 3-31 the wrenches are on the lower bolt and the locking nuts are in the split in the casting. The locking nut can be used in either of two ways.

If tightened to the left-side casting after tension with the bolt has been applied, it will lock the adjusting bolt into its present position.

If the bolt is loosened off and the nut driven to the right-side casting, it will spread the castings open. In this case, once the proper tension is established, the nut is held steady and the bolt is tightened to lock it in place. Holding the nut and turning the bolt will not move the casting inward.

## Rockwell

Fig 3-32

The two adjustment bolts on the Rockwell are housed in the casting bumps at the rear of the base. Fig. 3-32 shows a wrench on the upper bolt. The locking nuts can be seen inside the split casting. The locking nuts can be used in either of two ways.

If tightened to the left-side casting after having used the bolts to squeeze the castings in, they will lock the adjusting bolts into their present positions.

If the bolts are loosened off and the nuts driven to the right-side casting, they will spread the castings open. In this case, once the proper tension is established, the nuts are held steady and the bolts are tightened to lock it in place. Holding the nuts and turning the bolts will not move the castings inward.

# Column-to-Base: Rotation

The column must not rotate at all from side to side in the base. Slop here will make it impossible to maintain a straight cut later, for even if the arm is properly clamped to the column, it will still swing from side to side. A surprisingly small rotation can cause a large error at the end of the saw run. This is also the adjustment that wears most quickly, because the column is moved up and down often. Hence, it must be checked regularly.

The set screws which push against the column key control this rotation. Before testing and adjusting these set screws, you should be sure that the column and the column key are clean. Give the column key a little shot of WD-40. This is the only place in the whole machine where I really believe in regular light lubrication – but never with oil.

If you have just finished adjusting the base tension of the last section, your set screws will be completely backed off and the column will be rotating freely in the base. In this case, skip the test procedure, go to the adjustments, then come back to test again.

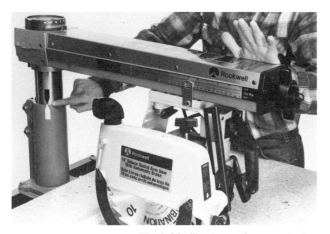

Fig 3-33 *Testing column rotation*

In Fig. 3-33 I am pointing at two arrows, a back one attached to the column and a white one attached to the base. The point where these arrows meet is the place to check for column-to-base rotation. You don't have to put two arrows on your machine. Watching the dust on the column and nearby dust on the base can provide the same reference points.

Watch closely at the junction between the column and the base and then shove the arm left and then right. You should see no movement at all at the column/base junction. You may prefer to put your finger at the junction point so that you can feel both the column and the base. You will clearly feel any movement as you push the arm back and forth.

There is enough flex in the arm that the end of the arm will move right and left even if there is no movement at the base. Don't let this worry you; we'll deal with it later.

In all three machines, the column-key set screws can add a bit of drag to the sliding tension between the column and the base. This can be used positively to add the last little bit of tension if the base was adjusted just slightly on the loose side in the last section. It can also unknowingly be the cause of the sliding tension becoming too tight, resulting in poor movement of the column. Always repeat the lowering of the arm test of the last section after adjusting the column key set screws.

## Craftsman

Fig 3-34

The Craftsman has two set screws that can be adjusted with an Allen key as shown in Fig. 3-34. These screws are tension fit and have no locking nuts.

Push the arm to the left to move the column key away from the set screws. Then tighten them both in snugly, and back them off the smallest fraction. Test both for rotation and downward travel.

## DeWalt

Fig 3-35

The DeWalt has two brass set screws which bear directly against the column key. They are locked into place by lock nuts. Fig. 3-35 shows a wrench on the locking nut and the Allen key in the set screw. As the set screw is made of brass, the column key is protected against wear but requires more frequent adjustment as the screws wear rather quickly. You must also be careful not to use either the Allen key or the wrench on the locking nut too forcefully or you will break the screw right off.

Push the arm to the left to move the column key away from the set screws. Then tighten them both in snugly, and back them off the smallest fraction. Test both for rotation and downward travel.

## Rockwell

Fig 3-36

The Rockwell has four set screws which bear against the column key. They serve the dual purpose of controlling column rotation and adjusting the travel of the saw square to the fence. At this point, they should be adjusted to prevent rotation of the column, even though we will come back and play with them again when we get to squaring up the machine.

The set screws are adjusted with an Allen wrench as seen in Fig. 3-36 and locked into place with a nut. Be careful not to force either the Allen wrench or the nut too tightly or you could break off the head of the screw.

# Crank Control

Some DeWalts have a belt drive that connects the crank to the column drive screw. This is a toothed belt which gives a reliable transmission of rotations from the crank to the column but it can loosen, causing either excessive slop in the crank handle or even jumping of the drive wheels from tooth to tooth.

Fig 3-37 *Belt drive*

To tighten the belt you must remove the cover on the arm. Then loosen the screws at both ends of the mounting bracket which holds the front belt wheel (on the crank handle shaft). With a second screwdriver up through the arm casting, wedge the mounting bracket forward, applying tension to the belt. Tighten the mounting screws.

Make sure that the set screw which attaches the crank handle onto its shaft is seated down tightly. This simple set screw is often the cause of what appears to be a lot of slop in the crank rotation.

The DeWalt has index marks around the crank handle to allow the use of the column drive screw for precise depth measurements. Precision is possible despite some play in a belt drive or some play in the right-angle gear drives of the Craftsman or the Rockwell, and despite ordinary play in the column drive screw itself by using the "end point of play" as described in Chapter 2.

### Rockwell

Place the arm so that it is somewhat square to the fence (don't bother too much with "square" yet). Snug the two bottom screws up to the column key. Then tighten the two upper ones. Test both for rotation and, as discussed in the last section, for column fall.

## Table-to-Arm: Parallel Planes

Fig 3-38 *Crank indexing*

The Craftsman and Rockwell machines have no provisions for measuring crank rotations, so by adding a simple marked disc under the table as shown in Fig. 3-38 you can enjoy this convenient feature. Verify your own machines, but generally one rotation of the crank on a Craftsman machine will raise or lower the blade by $1/16''$ while one rotation of the crank on a DeWalt or a Rockwell will move the blade $1/8''$.

With the large crank handles and radial indexing marks, it is quite easy to measure an eighth or even a sixteenth of a rotation of the handle – hence my promised one 128th of an inch accuracy. It really does work, if you have cleaned and adjusted the machine as explained so far in this book and you move in one direction: up to a starting point and then on up, or down to a starting point and then on down.

For dado cuts, it means simply holding the wood firmly against the table, lowering the saw with the blade operating until it just thinks about touching the top surface of the wood, pushing the saw back off the wood and then counting the rotations for the precise depth of dado cut you wish.

Up to this point we have done a great deal of work cleaning the machine and adjusting the tension. This was to ensure that as we begin to square things up, they remain square and operate square while cutting wood. Although certain variations in the order of squaring up are permissible, many of the adjustments affect other adjustments and hence must be carried out in the proper order. If you square up the whole machine and then change the table top, what is the saw square to?

The table is the starting point for all squaring operations. It is of capital importance that it be very flat, and that it be exactly parallel to the plane defined by the swing of the arm. If the table were to drop in the front with respect to the arm, the saw blade would tend to rise out of the wood as it came forward – a frustrating cut when making dados. All squaring adjustments are made to the table. If, at some later point, you accidentally or intentionally change the position of the table (dropping the machine, hammering on the table, changing the top, adding accessory tables), then you must return and recheck all squaring adjustments. This is why Procedure 2 dealt with completely assembling and covering the table top. This is why you should not follow the manufacturers' instructions that tell you to line up the table rails and then attach the table.

First, we must understand something about the plane of the arm. It is true that there is a certain flex in the column and the arm, causing the front end of the arm to drop slightly when the motor is pulled forward. However, when working with a sharp saw blade and moving the saw smoothly and without rushing, the saw will not ride up on the wood and the weight of the motor will always pull the arm down in the same manner. This is to say that although there is some flex, it is very consistent. For this reason you will want to adjust the table surface to be exactly parallel to the plane of the arm under its normal load, i.e., the weight of the motor.

To accomplish this, use the motor itself as your measuring instrument and arrange the arm in such a manner as to permit swinging it to the right and left without pushing it up and down with your hand.

# Locking Tongue Open

The indexing pin (or tongue) which drops into the column to hold the arm at 90° or 45° will cause trouble when lining up the table because every time you want to swing the arm you will have to pull hard against the spring. This has a tendency to pull the front end of the arm down, which causes a discrepancy in the setting of the parallel planes. Hence, the first step is to jam it into the "open" position, enabling you to push gently on the side of the arm (pushing neither up nor down) allowing it to swing without stopping to any desired position over the table top.

**Craftsman**

Fig 3-39

**DeWalt**

Fig 3-40

**Rockwell**

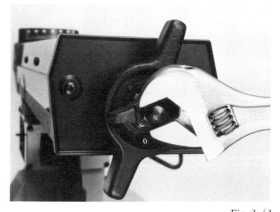

Fig 3-41

## Craftsman

A small wooden wedge made of $^3/_8''$ wood can be placed behind the locking handle as shown in Fig. 3-39. This will prevent the handle from returning and hence hold the tongue away from the column.

## DeWalt

A small wooden wedge made of $^3/_8''$ wood can be placed behind the locking handle as shown in Fig. 3-40. This will prevent the handle from returning and hence will hold the tongue away from the column.

## Rockwell

On the Rockwell, there are two large wing-nut-type handles on the front end of the arm. The smaller one pulls the index-ing tongue out of the column. Back it out all the way, and if necessary give the end nut (being held by the wrench in Fig. 3-41) a very slight over-tightening. This will generally hold the pin out and leave the arm free to swing.

   If the above procedure doesn't want to work without forc-ing the end nut, then remove the miter scale disc as shown in Fig. 3-42. This will automatically release the pressure on the springs that force the tongue into the column. The arm will now swing freely.

Fig 3-42

# Positioning Table Rails

On all three machines, each rail is attached to the base with two large bolts. Tighten them all up snug but not too tight, positioning them about midway in their adjustable slots.

Remove the saw blade and turn the motor so that the shaft points downward toward the table. Follow the next steps exactly and you will have the table rails adjusted very quickly. Any other procedure can take you hours since every change you make changes the one you made before.

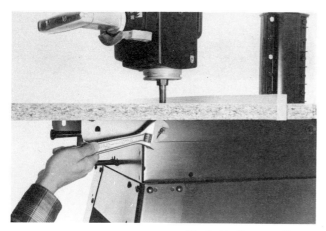

Fig 3-43 *Front rail nuts*

Fig. 3-43 shows a crescent wrench on the front rail nut and the motor shaft almost in contact with the table directly above this front rail nut. Swing the motor shaft to the position directly above the other front rail nut. Determine which of the two is the highest and then tighten down that nut.

Now return the motor so that it is positioned directly over the lower front rail nut. With the crescent wrench held as shown, slowly lift the wrench handle. This will tend to tighten the nut. At the same time the head of the wrench will wedge between the nut and the table rail, forcing the rail upward in a very controlled manner. Lift until the table-top surface is the same distance from the motor shaft as it was for the other front nut. The blade wrench can be used as a feeler gauge between the motor shaft and the table top if you are unsure of your visual sighting.

So far, you only have two points of the table in the plane parallel to the arm. But the important thing is that these two points are pivot points for the rear adjustment, meaning that they will not change when you adjust the rear of the table. If you had tried to set the height of the front edge of the table, it would have dropped down when the rear end was raised.

Fig 3-44 *Rear rail nuts*

Now swing the motor to the rear of the table just above one of the rails as in Fig. 3-44. If this part of the table is too high, loosen the rear bolt (as shown in Fig. 3-44) and slightly lower the table so that it is a bit too low. Then put the wrench in the position of Fig. 3-43 and raise the rail until the top surface of the table is the same distance from the motor shaft as in

# Flattening the Table

the previous adjustments. Do the same thing with the rear end of the other rail.

You should now have four points on the table that are exactly the same distance from the motor shaft and hence in the same plane. Tighten all four nuts down very securely. Now recheck that each of these four points is the same distance from the motor shaft when the motor is placed directly above each point.

The center of the table may be at exactly the correct position (the same distance from the motor shaft as above the rails) or it could be warped, making it either higher or lower.

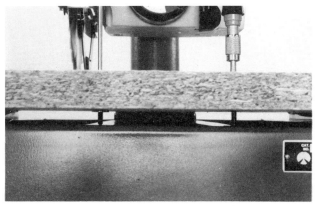

Fig 3-45 *Table center*

The Craftsman and the Rockwell have adjustment screws to compensate for this. In Fig. 3-45 you can see two screws between the table and the base (I have put screwdrivers above each of them). One of these screws will pull the table down toward the base, the other will push it up away from the base. Do not tighten both of them or you will create an "S" shaped table. Use the motor shaft to determine if you need to go up or down and adjust accordingly.

The DeWalt has no adjustment for this. Although I have never found one of their tables bent upwards, they often do bend downwards. This can easily be compensated for with a cedar shingle as a wedge, pushing the table up toward the motor shaft. A more sophisticated solution would be a wood screw through the base into the table to pull it down or a machine screw with a spacing nut through the base to the table to force it upward.

The above adjustments should have put the entire table into a plane quite flat and parallel to the travel of the overhead arm. Let me add one caution, however. If you hang extension wings on the table, over the long run they will tend to bend the outside edges of the table down and curve the whole surface. See my support precautions for this in Chapter 6.

## Planing Table Flat

The wood on your table may not be absolutely flat, or the center screws may have created a slight "mountain" in the center (making it quite difficult to align the blade 90° to the table). The perfectionist will want to "machine" or "plane" the table absolutely flat.

Fig 3-47 *Arbor nuts*

Fig 3-46 *Planing table*

This can be accomplished by using a rigid sanding disc attachment available for all machines. Drop it to the surface, starting in the back of the table, and without raising or lowering the arm with the force of your hand, carefully push it from side to side. Don't forget to tighten the rip lock so that it won't move on the arm, and take a very, very light cut. The sanding disc is 6″ in diameter but can only efficiently sand on half of its surface, 3″ at a time. Move forward in 3″ increments as shown in Fig. 3-46. This will perfectly plane all the table with the exception of the two front corners, which you will have to finish off by hand (however these are relatively unimportant for the operation of the saw).

All three machines use arbor nuts that have one side slightly rounded off. The other side has what looks like a washer machined into the nut itself. Although it may make no difference on your saw, the machined surface is the one that is certain to be square to the threads. This is important when attaching accessories such as the sanding disc since it is the pressure of the disc against this machined surface that eliminates wobble in the disc.

This means that when attaching saw blades, the machined surface of the nut goes in toward the blade. When mounting attachments like the sanding disc which go on the end of the shaft, the nut is put on the shaft first with its machined surface out towards the attachment.

## Blade Square to Table (Rough)

Before attempting to square the blade to the table, you must first check that the table is flat. If it has a high spot or a valley in the middle, you will be squaring the blade to one side of the table and not to the way the wood may lie when resting on your uneven table. If the table is not perfectly flat, return to Procedure 6 and solve the problem before proceeding.

We are going to square the blade to both the table and the fence in two different steps. The first (rough) squaring is done quickly, just to get in the right ball park. This then allows us to properly align the heel and toe, a necessary step before proceeding to precision squaring of the machine. If you know your machine to be fairly square already, you can skip Procedures 7 and 8.

Unplug the machine. Lock the arm clamp to the column. Lock the carriage yoke clamp. Attach a saw blade to the motor and leave the guard off. Lock the rip clamp in the position shown in Fig. 3-48. Release the bevel clamp and wiggle the motor up and down to ensure that the indexing pin is seated all the way in the 90° position. Now force the motor lightly in a clockwise direction (lifting the saw blade) and lock the bevel clamp.

These steps will ensure that the entire machine is rigid and that you are on the end point of any play that may perhaps exist in your bevel indexing pin. Pushing the motor clockwise is important as this is the direction that the action of cutting in wood will tend to push the blade. However, it will not be able to move in that direction because you are on the end point of play.

Fig 3-48 *Testing square to table (rough)*

Using a framing square as shown in Fig. 3-48, check to see if the blade is reasonably square to the table. Be sure to place the square in between the off-set teeth of the blade so that you can compare the square leg directly against the saw blade.

Rotate the saw blade about one third of a turn and check again, and then another third. Saw blades are often slightly wobbly and this can easily send you off adjusting in the wrong direction. In fact, this blade wobble is one of the reasons that a square is not used in Procedure 11, where the blade will be set precisely square to the table.

For now, fairly square is good enough.

Allow me a little aside on how to check if your framing square is square. Use the long leg of the square to locate a very straight edge (on a piece of wood or a counter top). Hold the short leg in your left hand and hook it on that straight edge. Draw a line away from that straight edge along the other leg. Now flip the square over so that the short leg is in your right hand. Hook it on the straight edge again and draw a line along the long leg on top of the first pencil line. If the two lines are identical, your square is square. If they spread out from each other, your square is not square.

Framing squares can be brought back into square by hitting them in the right place with a metal punch: just above the inside corner to open the angle and just inside the outside corner to close the angle.

With all that said and done, all we really need to set up a radial arm saw dead square is a good straight edge and a tape measure and not a square at all. Remember what I said in Chapter 2 about "verifications on cut wood"?

**Craftsman**

Fig 3-49

**DeWalt**

Fig 3-50

**Rockwell**

Fig 3-51

To adjust the 90° bevel indexing point square to the table on the Rockwell, you must remove the bevel indicating

## Travel Square to Fence (Rough)

### Craftsman

In order to adjust the 90° bevel indexing point square to the table on the Craftsman, you must first remove the handle. In Fig. 3-49 you can see an Allen wrench in one of the four Allen screws that hold this adjustment. Loosen all four so that the motor can be rotated, but not so much as to cause the blade to fall to the table. Rotate the motor until the saw blade is in line with the framing square. Then very gently tighten up the screws, a little at a time, moving around as you would to tighten the head of an automobile motor. If you simply tighten the first one up hard, it will tend to rotate the motor and you will lose your adjustment. Make the rounds and tighten each screw a little, then firmly and finally tight.

### DeWalt

To adjust the 90° bevel indexing point square to the table on the DeWalt, you must first remove the little bevel-indicator plate. Fig. 3-50 shows you the location of three large Allen screws. The center one can generally be left alone unless the motor is too easy or too hard to rotate. The other two must be loosened, the motor rotated to the proper position and then retightened. Do not tighten one up hard while the other is still loose or the motor will rotate with your action. Tighten each one a little bit, then firmly and finally tight.

### Rockwell

plate. As this will also remove the indexing pin, be sure that you have followed the procedures outlined in the test section of this procedure. More specifically, loosen the bevel clamp handle, push the bevel indexing pin in hard, rotate the motor clockwise against any play in the indexing position and then lock down the bevel clamp.

You will find four hex bolts and one Allen screw as shown in Fig. 3-51. The Allen screw need not be touched unless the motor is too hard or too easy to turn. Loosen just slightly the four bolts and adjust the motor so that the blade is in line with the leg of the framing square. Tighten up the bolts. They must be tightened a little at a time, one at a time, or the act of tightening them will change the adjustment.

In this procedure, we will adjust the travel of the carriage roughly square to the fence. The blade itself could well be quite unsquare to the fence even when the travel is square as we have not yet taken care of the heel and toe adjustments. Essentially, what we will do here is ensure that the arm is square to the fence. It is only for convenience that we use the saw blade to accomplish this.

We will be working with the saw blade mounted on the motor but with no guard, so make sure the machine is not plugged into an electrical outlet. The bevel clamp, the yoke clamp and the arm clamp should all be tight.

Fig 3-52 *Testing square to fence (rough)*

Raise the saw blade so that it is just barely above the table top. Place the framing square against the fence close enough to the blade to barely touch one tooth, causing a faint but clear metal-on-metal scraping sound. Hold the blade still with your thumb as shown in Fig. 3-52. That will prevent the blade from climbing up on the square while moving forward. Now draw the saw forward, being careful not to force left or right with your arm.

If the sound is even all the way along, the travel is roughly square. If the saw binds into the square you will need to adjust to the right. If the sound stops because the blade has drifted to the right, the arm must be brought back to the left.

Before attempting any of the following adjustments for the arm, loosen the arm-to-column clamp while leaving the indexing tongue in place and see if the arm can move in the direction required. If so, reclamp at the new position and try again. If roughly square lies anywhere within the slop of the arm index point, that is good enough for now; you can skip to the next procedure.

## Craftsman

Fig 3-53

## DeWalt

Fig 3-54

## Rockwell

Prior to adjusting the Rockwell for carriage travel square to the fence, you should check to see if the sliding tension is correct on the arm-to-column indexing tongue. Release the arm-to-column clamp and move the arm from side to side. If it moves a great deal, the tongue tension should be increased. If the tongue fails to drop easily into its indexing position, the tongue tension should be released a bit. There are two Allen adjustment screws located in the left side of the arm just in front of the column. The arm should be pulled toward the left side while the indexing tongue is in its slot to take pressure off the screws, and the screws slightly adjusted as necessary.

To adjust the Rockwell for carriage travel square to the fence, you must work with four set screws located in the

## Craftsman

The position of the arm with respect to the fence on the Craftsman is controlled by means of three Allen screws at the back of the arm as shown in fig. 3-53. These three screws simply clamp the indexing ring down to the column. When you release them, you will lose all reference as to where your last adjustment was, so do it carefully and move the arm carefully. Once moved, they must be locked down hard before trying to test the travel again.

The Craftsman has no adjustment for the tension on the arm-to-column indexing pin. When it gets loose there is nothing you can do to tighten it, but Procedure 10 will show you how to compensate for any slop here.

## DeWalt

The position of the arm with respect to the fence on the DeWalt is controlled by two screws which bear against opposite sides of the arm-to-column indexing tongue. Fig. 3-54 shows a screwdriver on one of the screws while there is an Allen key on the set screw which locks the adjustments from underneath. There is a second identical pair on the other side of the arm.

First, a few notes on these screws themselves. There is a tiny brass plug located between the locking set screw and the main adjustment screw. DeWalt puts these brass plugs on all its locking set screws to protect the threads of the primary adjustment screw as well to enable infinite adjustment (if the set screw were permitted to cut into the threads of the adjusting screw, it would tend to always "home back" to the first dent). Don't lose the plugs! You will also notice that these adjustment screws have a hole in the center of the screw driver slot. This is intended to receive the "straw" of a WD-40 can, allowing light lubrication of the arm-to-column indexing tongue.

To adjust the DeWalt arm, loosen both set screws, tighten both adjustment screws and then back one of them off just a fraction of a turn. *Retighten the set screws*. Test the tongue release lever (arm clamping lever) to see if the tongue moves freely in and out. If you fail to retighten the set screws before every test of the release lever, the opening action itself will turn one or both of the adjusting screws and you will lose your adjustment. If the two adjustment screws bear too tightly against this tongue, it will not seat properly into its indexing position. You must allow it a little slop, but we will eliminate the effect of that slop in Procedure 10.

## Rockwell

Fig 3-55

back of the base. Fig. 3-55 shows an Allen key near the lower right-hand screw. The other side has two identical screws. Each set screw has a locking nut. These are the same screws that we previously adjusted to eliminate column-to-base rotation (Procedure 5 to 5.4). Review that section to assure yourself that any changes you make here will not introduce any column-to-base rotation, nor interfere with the column rise and fall.

Loosen all four lock nuts. Back off the two lower set screws. We will make the alignment adjustments with the upper pair and then bring the lower ones in to match at the end.

Loosen slightly the set screw on the side where the arm is running away from the square. Push the arm into square

## Heel and Toe

### DeWalt

Now test for square travel to the fence. If you must move the arm, release both of the set screws and loosen the adjustment screw on the side moving away from square. If the saw moves to the right of square, loosen the right adjustment screw. If the saw moves to the left of square, loosen the left adjustment screw. Loosen the adjustment screw only a fraction of a turn. Now push the arm in the direction you want it to go and then tighten the other adjustment screw the same fraction of a turn that you loosened the first one. By moving both screws the same amount, you will maintain exactly the same tension on the indexing tongue but you will effectively move the arm over. It moves away from the screw you loosen and towards the screw you tighten.

Don't forget to retighten the set screws before playing with the locking/index lever.

### Rockwell

and tighten the other set screw by exactly the same amount of rotation that you used in loosening the first set screw. This will keep the same tension on the column key. The arm will move toward the set screw being tightened and away from the set screw being loosened. Tighten down the locknuts on these two set screws to that they will not turn while testing. Be careful not to force the Allen wrench or the locking nut as you can easily break these little screws. Test that the column still moves up and down correctly. Test the carriage travel to the fence. If it is still not square, adjust again and test again.

When everything is working correctly, bring in the lower two set screws, snug but not too tight. Lock their nuts down. Test again for column rotation and rise and fall.

It would be nice to take a break and dance a bit, but no, when we talk about "heel" and "toe" in a saw we are talking about the leading cutting edge of the blade (the toe) and the tailing edge where the back of the blade last emerges from the wood (the heel). If the front and the back of the blade are not perfectly lined up with the travel of the saw, the back of the blade will make a second and usually ragged cut on the wood off to one side. This twisted blade position is often referred to as "heeling".

To understand this more clearly, rotate the yoke of your saw halfway between a cross cut and a rip cut. With the arm in its usual cross cut position, imagine drawing the saw forward into a piece of wood. It would make a pretty strange cut if it would cut at all. In reality our saws are never so far off. In fact, the error is usually less than the width of the set of the teeth. It is for this reason that it cuts anyway and we never stop to ask if there was some way to stop that bloody splintering on the backside of the cut. Few people realize that good table saws also have adjustments for heel and toe alignment. If the blade is not parallel to the miter gauge slot, you're in trouble.

Since the radial arm saw works in the horizontal as well as the vertical position, we must adjust the heel and the toe of both positions. You say you never use the horizontal position? If you cut an ordinary 45° bevel, you're using half of the adjustments from the horizontal position and half the adjustments from the vertical position.

There are various valid techniques for testing the heel and toe alignment. I have developed a very simple jig that is surprisingly precise because it works on the principle of using the saw blade as a sounding board. See Fig. 3-56. As you spin the blade backwards with a flip of your hand, the saw teeth barely graze the ends of the dowels on the jig. The resulting ringing sound can detect the slightest wobble in the saw blade and misalignment of heel and toe that you would be hard pressed to measure with calipers. Students in my seminars can hear one 128th of an inch misalignment from the back of the room.

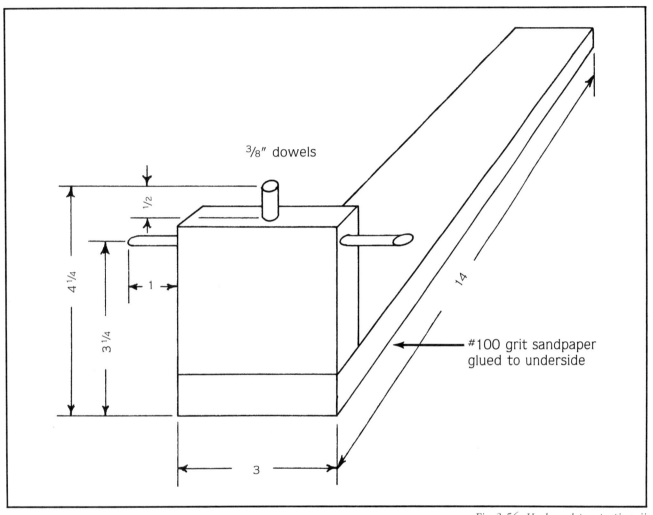

³/₈″ dowels

¹/₂

4¹/₄

3¹/₄

1

3

14

#100 grit sandpaper
glued to underside

Fig 3-56 *Heel and toe testing jig*

With all three machines, it is important to adjust the horizontal heel and toe before the vertical. Although all three are quite different, the horizontal adjustments can affect the vertical adjustments in each machine, the vertical adjustments have no effect on the horizontal ones.

Before making any tests or adjustments, loosen the yoke clamp and wiggle the yoke (twisting left and right) to assure that the yoke indexing pin is well seated into its hole. Now twist it to the right and lock down the clamp. This will ensure that if there is any play in the pin you will be using the end point of play as discussed in Chapter 2.

# Horizontal Heel and Toe

To test horizontal heel and toe alignment, the machine should be unplugged. A saw blade should be mounted on the motor and the guard left off. Put the saw into the horizontal position and tighten all clamps.

Fig 3-57 *Testing horizontal heel and toe*

Place the jig on the table just left of center a couple of inches out from the fence as shown in Fig. 3-57. Drop the blade down and move the carriage so that the tips of the saw teeth just barely scratch the very top of the dowel in the jig. With a flick of your wrist, spin the saw blade backwards (so the teeth won't bite into the jig). Lower the blade until one or more teeth "sing out". Then with the blade still spinning, pull the saw forward so that the teeth at the rear of the blade are just over the dowel (the jig has not moved). If the "singing" stops, the heel is too high. If the "singing" is stronger, or the teeth grind into the jig, the heel is too low. Note whether the *heel* was too high or too low as we will adjust the heel, not the toe.

**Craftsman**

Fig 3-58

**DeWalt**

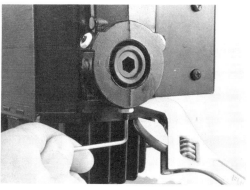

Fig 3-59

**Rockwell**

Fig 3-60

## Craftsman

On the Craftsman, the horizontal heel is adjusted at the back motor mounting of the yoke. First release the bevel clamp up front. Then slightly loosen the mounting nut seen in Fig. 3-58. The strange looking washer behind the nut is eccentric. Turning it with a screw driver will raise or lower the back side of the motor, and hence the heel of the saw blade.

You will notice that the mounting bolt is a bit sloppy in its hole. It allows for the above adjustment, but at the same time will most likely change the position for the vertical heel and toe. Always recheck the vertical heel and toe (next section in the book) after any adjustment is made on this bolt.

Tighten the nut securely and run the test again.

## DeWalt

All heel and toe adjustments on the DeWalt are made at the back motor mounting. Fig. 3-59 shows the motor mounting shaft coming through the center of the yoke harness. There are three Allen adjusting screws which point toward the center with three locking nuts (painted white in the photo).

Loosen all the locking nuts. Back off the two upper adjusting screws (these are for adjusting the vertical heel and toe). Now you can raise or lower the adjusting screw which comes up through the bottom until the horizontal heel and toe is correct. Then tighten the lower locking nut.

The motor will pivot to the right or left for the vertical heel and toe adjustment, but that will not change the horizontal position. Every time you readjust the lower screw, you must recheck the vertical heel and toe.

## Rockwell

Rockwell has no horizontal heel and toe adjustment whatsoever. The machines I have seen have been reasonably in line, but if you must make an adjustment it can be done. You will have to remove the carriage from the arm. This will give you access to the roller wheels. As you can see in Fig. 3-60, you will have to add shim washers under two of the wheels.

If you must drop the heel of the blade, add shim washers under the two rear wheels. If you must raise the heel of the blade, add shim washers under the two forward wheels. The shim washers should be about half the thickness of the total lift or fall desired and they must not be so large in diameter as to rub on the outer race of the wheel. These shims will most likely be thin enough so as not to seriously bother the alignment of the four carriage rollers with respect to the arm track. The difficulty is, of course, that you have to put it all back together again to test it.

# Vertical Heel and Toe

To test vertical heel and toe alignment, the saw should be unplugged and a blade mounted with no guard. The miter, bevel and yoke clamps should all be secured. The blade should be slightly above the table surface.

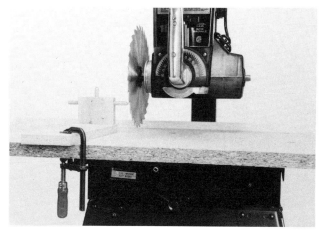

Fig 3-61  *Testing vertical heel and toe*

Place the heel and toe testing jig to the left of the blade travel and a couple of inches from the fence as shown in Fig. 3-61. Clamp it to the front end of the table. Now place the tips of the saw teeth just beside the dowel sticking out on the side of the jig. With a flick of your wrist, spin the blade backward and gently tap the jig over toward the blade until the saw blade begins to "sing". One or more teeth will begin to ring out.

With the blade still spinning backward, pull the saw forward until the teeth on the back of the blade are alongside the jig dowel. If there is no sound, your heel is off to the right. If the sound is stronger or the blade jams into the dowel, your heel is off to the left.

**Craftsman**

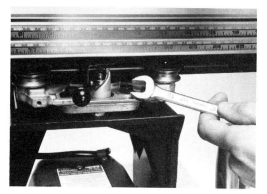

Fig 3-62

**DeWalt**

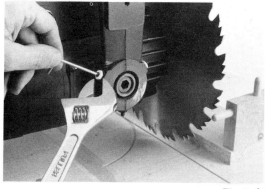

Fig 3-63

**Rockwell**

Fig 3-64

## Travel Square to Fence (Precision)

### Craftsman

In order to adjust the vertical heel and toe on the Craftsman, you must remove the left-side wheel cover to expose two hex bolts as seen in Fig. 3-62. These should be loosened just slightly and the entire yoke assembly swung right or left to correct the heel and toe. Don't loosen them too much or the whole assembly will move a great deal and you will lose track of the adjustment you wanted to make. Tighten them up and test again.

### DeWalt

To adjust the vertical heel and toe alignment on the DeWalt, loosen the two locking nuts holding the two angled Allen adjustment screws as shown in Fig. 3-64. Then loosen one of the screws a fraction of a turn and drive the other one up tight. Test for heel again and continue moving the rear motor mount left or right as necessary. Finally tighten down the locking nuts.

Do not touch the bottom screw unless you want to adjust the horizontal heel and toe. Note that the motor mounting pivots on the bottom screw, so playing with the top two has no effect on the bottom adjustment.

### Rockwell

To adjust vertical heel and toe on the Rockwell, locate the two hex head bolts on either side of the indexing pin under the yoke. See Fig. 3-64. First release the yoke clamp. Then loosen the two bolts just slightly. If you loosen them too much, you will lose track of the adjustment you wanted to make. Swing the entire carriage left or right to straighten out the heel and then retighten the two bolts. Test again to verify the adjustment.

Now you will begin to feel as if you are getting somewhere. For the precision adjustments, we will mount a saw blade on the motor shaft, install the guard and plug the machine in. As we make our final adjustments we want to judge the machine by how it cuts wood, not by some square that is more or less square and perhaps a bit flexible.

First, we must master the technique for measuring precisely 90° from the fence. Then we must see how to add precision to the adjustment techniques outlined in Procedure 8.

# Precision Testing

For precision testing, you need a board 10″ to 12″ wide and about 24″ long. Pressboard or plywood ¾ in thickness would be the least expensive and the flattest. This board must have both long edges very straight and parallel to each other. Check for straightness with a straight edge. To check that the edges are parallel, simply measure the width with a tape or a ruler, verifying that the board has the same width from one end to the other. Once your saw is operating perfectly, make up some test boards in advance, as you will want to test it regularly.

Fig 3-66 *Testing, second cut*

Fig 3-65 *Testing, first cut*

Now you must reverse the test board. Lift the front end and put it against the fence (do not move the left side to the right). The first cut will now be against the table surface. Line up this cut with the pencil marks you just made on the table. This will ensure that the second cut of the saw will end up perfectly in line with the first cut on this edge of the board as shown in Fig. 3-66. Make the second cut.

Adjust the height of the saw so that it will cut barely half way through your test board. For purposes of demonstrating how this test works, set your miter angle to about 5°. This will ensure us a cut that is clearly not square to the fence. Place the test board tightly against the fence and draw the saw all the way across the board. Without moving the board, use a pencil to mark the table just below where the saw came through the wood as shown in Fig. 3-65.

Fig 3-67  *Testing, divergent*

Fig. 3-67 shows the test board with a mirror in the back to allow us to see both the front and rear edge of the board at the same time. In the front, the two cuts match perfectly. This will be true if the saw is square or not because we lined them up with the pencil marks on the table. But the back side will always show us twice the error of the saw. On our 12″ test board we see the divergence from square that would occur if we had made a cross cut 24″ long.

Fig 3-68  *Testing, wide shoulder*

Fig. 3-68 shows the same operation but with the saw close to being square. The top and bottom cuts are directly in line with each other all the way across the wood, so the board is severed. In this photo there is a fairly wide shoulder. With a wide shoulder, it is not easy to be sure if the machine is really precisely square.

## Precision Adjustments

Move the left piece in and cut again so that there is little or no shoulder. If the shoulder is perfectly even the full length of the cut, the saw is cutting square to the fence.

Fig 3-69 *Testing, narrow shoulder*

Fig. 3-69 shows the cut with barely any shoulder. When the top and bottom cuts are this close to each other, the slightest divergence is easily visible. We want to adjust the arm until all cuts are reliably this close – every time.

To adjust the travel of the cut square to the fence in order to satisfy the above test, you must use the techniques described in Procedure 8. But in that section I only showed where the adjustment screws were and how to manipulate them to get a rough alignment.

The biggest problem we have with the arm is that after all efforts have been made to eliminate rotation in the column and any other play all along the whole machine, we are stuck with the fact that the arm-to-column indexing tongue often leaves a bit of play. In theory, you can adjust this so that the end of the arm will move little more than $1/8''$ left and right. In practice, we don't need to work so hard.

First, we must verify that the only slop left in the machine is in fact that indexing tongue. Pull the saw to the front of the table with the blade barely above the table top. Clamp everything down tight, even the rip clamp which fixes the carriage to the arm. Push the arm to the right and then release it. With a pencil, mark the point on the table directly below the blade. Now push the arm to the left and release it. It should still be above the same point on the table with no variation. If there is any variation, return to the previous chapters to determine what is not properly tightened. It will probably be the column keyway adjustments.

Once the problem is solved, release the arm-to-column clamp and repeat the test. Now there may be as much as half an inch difference between the two points. That is the play in the arm-to-column tongue.

There are two things to note here. First, when the arm-to-column clamp is engaged, there is no play. Second, if you move the arm to 30°, then back to square and wiggle the arm a bit to be sure that the tongue is well seated, it always comes back to exactly the same place. It will still have the same slop, but both ends of the slop will be at the same place every time. Try it.

# Miter Scales

Now we will use one of the principles of precision explained in Chapter 2, Principle 3. Every time you perform the precision testing technique:

- first swing the arm away from center;
- then bring the arm back to center;
- wiggle the arm left and right to ensure that the tongue is completely seated into the column;
- grasp the table with your right hand and the end of the arm with your left, force the arm to the right (the end of play);
- release the arm and clamp it securely to the column.

You have now securely positioned the arm on the extreme right of the only play remaining. This may not be square to the fence, but it is a position that you can come back to precisely and easily at any time. Now follow the adjustment procedures of Procedure 8 so that this end point of play is in fact exactly square to the fence. Adjust the arm. Lock down any locking screws or nuts. Swing the arm away from center. Return to center. Seat the tongue. Shove the arm to the right. Lock it to the column. Test.

Once the center position (I've been calling it 90° but in fact the miter scale will show it as 0°) has been precisely aligned, you will be happy to know that both 45° miter positions are automatically in the right place. All you have to do is to remember to push the arm to the right of the play in any of the indexed positions before clamping it to the column.

Why do I insist on shoving to the right and not the left? While cross cutting there is very little, if any, side pressure on the arm that would tend to move the arm from its clamped position. When you rip however, if you are feeding the wood with some pressure, that same pressure is working against the arm-to-column clamp. The out-rip position provides more leverage against this clamp than the in-rip position, so by seating the arm on the right side of the play in the indexing tongue, the clamp has nowhere to slip during out-rip operations. This is a simple extra security against the possible creation of a "rip heel and toe problem" (see Procedure 12).

The miter scales vary greatly in precision with none of them good enough to permit cutting without verifying the actual angle that will come out on the wood. Although 45° left, 0° and 45° right can be indexed quite precisely, all positions in between must be carefully tested on wood before executing the cut on a piece of furniture.

One way to line up an angle without cutting wood is to raise the saw blade just above the wood to be cut. Draw the saw along the wood and adjust the miter angle until one tooth of the saw blade exactly traces the angle marked on the surface of the wood. Then you can drop the blade and cut the miter.

Once the travel of the blade is perfectly square to the fence you can calibrate the miter scale on the back of the machine. This should be set to 0°.

## Craftsman

Fig 3-70

The Craftsman miter scale adjusts simply by placing a screw driver (or the end of the blade wrench as shown in Fig. 3-70) into the top of the scale and turning it until 0° lines up with the pointer.

## DeWalt

Fig 3-71

The DeWalt miter scale is calibrated by loosening the screws in the top of the scale and simply turning the scale itself until 0° lines up with the left side of the pointer. After lining up dozens of DeWalt machines, I must say that I have not yet found one that measures within 2° on the miter scale. They index perfectly, but the miter scale will read something like 47° when the machine is cutting at 45°. If you have this problem, don't fret; it's the machine and not you. The problem is that the scale is not properly centered on the column. But since we can't rely too closely on the miter scales anyway, it's not worth trying to fix it yourself.

## Rockwell

Fig 3-72

The miter scale on the Rockwell is calibrated by loosening the screw which holds the pointer and sliding it from side to side until it points directly at 0°.

## Blade Square to Table (Precision)

## Precision Testing

To adjust the blade precisely square to the table you must first verify that you have a flat table (otherwise, which part of the table are you square to?) Mount a saw blade and the guard and plug the machine in.

You will see how to make precision tests for square and then how to make precision adjustments.

There are several reasons why a framing square will not be used for precision testing of the blade-to-table angle. First of all, blades often have a bit of wobble in them. These blades can cut wood dead square despite wobble; they just make a slightly wider kerf cut. But if you try to square this blade to the table with a framing square, which part of the wobble will you use? Secondly, you want to square the dynamic action of the saw in motion to the table. That is, what really counts is that the wood you cut comes out perfectly square. Here is a simple procedure that takes all these variations into account.

You will need a very straight or flat table and a piece of wood $3/4''$ to $1^1/2''$ thick, $3''$ wide and $18''$ to $24''$ long. This wood must be very straight and its two edges must be exactly parallel to each other. Check for straightness with a straight edge. Measure across the face from edge to edge. If this dimension is exactly the same the whole length of the board, the two edges are parallel.

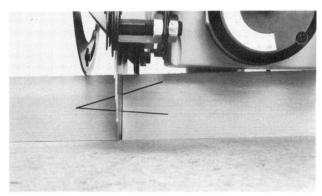

Fig 3-73 *Testing, cutting through*

Just to see clearly how this test procedure works, set your saw to a 5° bevel. That will make it visibly out of square. Mark one face of the wood with a "V", stand the board up on edge against the fence and carefully cut through as in Fig. 3-73. The wood is marked with a "V" so as not to lose track of the orientation of the two halves of the board.

## Precision Adjustments

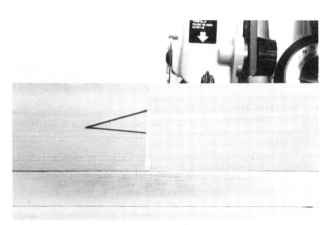

Fig 3-74 *Testing, reverse one side*

Remove the two halves from the saw and stand them on edge on a very straight surface, placed exactly as they were in the saw. Now take the right half and turn it onto its other edge as shown in Fig. 3-74 (don't turn it end for end). If the saw was not cutting square to the table you will see a "V" gap between the two boards. The size of this gap shows twice the error of the blade. The boards will only fit perfectly together in both the first and the second positions if the cut is perfectly square.

By doubling the cut (you have two cuts each 3″ high) you are in fact measuring the precision of the bevel angle on 6″ of cut – twice the capacity of the machine. Make any necessary adjustments and then test again.

To adjust the blade square to the table in order to satisfy the above test you must use the techniques described in Procedure 7. However, in that section I only showed where the adjustment screws were and how to manipulate them to get a rough alignment.

First we must handle any play that may exist in the bevel indexing pin. Loosen the bevel clamp handle. Grasp the blade guard and wiggle the motor up and down to ensure that the spring-loaded bevel-indexing pin seats properly all the way into its indexing hole. Now lift the guard upward (twisting the motor clockwise). Close the bevel clamp while holding the motor up in this position. You have just placed the bevel on the end point of any play that may have existed in its indexing mechanism. We use the clockwise end point of play position because the motor generally tends to want to lift upward, so the indexing pin, rather than the clamp, holds it in place.

If, in this position, it fails the precision test explained above, you will need to make bevel adjustments as explained in Procedure 7. Remember to loosen the bolts just slightly or the motor will slump downward, losing any reference points established before the attempted adjustment. When retightening the bolts, tighten each one alternately, a little at a time so that your wrench does not change the adjustment you just made.

# Bevel Scales

On all three machines the bevel scales are more accurate than the miter scales. They can almost be relied on. But "almost" means that you should always verify the angle that a setting cuts in wood before continuing with your construction project. The two 45° index points are, however, quite precise. Just remember to seat the indexing pin first, then force slightly clockwise and clamp down the position. If it is square at 0°, it will be dead on at 45°.

Square to the table is considered to be 0° bevel. All three machines calibrate the bevel scale by simply loosening the holding screw or screws on the pointer and setting it to 0°.

**Craftsman**

Fig 3-75

**DeWalt**

Fig 3-76

**Rockwell**

Fig 3-77

## Rip Heel and Toe

## Causes of Heeling

Rip heeling means that the front of the blade and the back of the blade are not exactly in line with the fence when the saw is in one of its rip positions. If the blade heels into the fence, the wood will bind and burn on the side closest to the fence and/or make a ragged cut on the fence side of the kerf. If the blade heels away from the fence the wood will tend to drift away from the fence while ripping and make a ragged cut on the side away from the fence.

There are four major culprits that can cause this heeling.

The most common is that few people ever adjust the heel and toe in the cross cut position. The heeling doesn't affect the work too seriously until you try to rip. I assume that you have already executed Procedure 9: heel and toe adjustment.

The second is that dust or chips are between the fence and the table, throwing the fence out of line with an otherwise square blade. Slide the fence back and forth to push the dust out before clamping it.

The third most common occurrence is that the arm is not square to the fence. If you have not taken care to make sure that the arm is exactly square to the fence, the saw will still cut boards with little problem in the cross cut position, but when swung over to the rip, the heeling starts to give serious trouble. Proper execution of Procedure 10 should permanently and easily eliminate this problem.

Lastly, the yoke indexing mechanism could be giving you problems.

The yoke indexing pin is usually quite precise on all machines. This is to say that if the cross cut is square to the fence and there is no heeling during a cross cut, swinging the saw around to either rip position will automatically ensure that it is perfectly lined up and ready to rip with precision.

Fig 3-78 *Marking yoke castings*

If there is any play, it is probably consistent with all four indexing points. In this case, simply be sure that every time you rotate the yoke, you twist to the right before clamping the yoke down to ensure that you are always on the "end point of play". If you have done this before adjusting the vertical heel and toe in Procedure 9, you will have automatically adjusted the heel and toe in both rip positions. In any case, always wiggle the yoke a little before applying the clamp to be sure that the indexing pin has had a chance to drop fully into place.

On some older Craftsman models, the indexing pin was so poorly designed that even twisting to the right would not guarantee being in the same place every time. To obtain consistent results with the cutting action of the saw on these machines, you will have to clamp the yoke into the correct position to eliminate heeling in the cross cut. Then make a permanent fine line mark across the two plates of the yoke indexing mechanism (again where the arrow is in Fig. 3-78). Then move to one of the rip positions and use the following test procedure to establish the correct position for eliminating heeling in this rip position. Clamp the yoke down in this position and mark the lower plate of the indexing mechanism to correspond to the mark that is already on the upper plate. Then shift to the other rip position; test, clamp and mark again. Now when you move from one position to another, do not rely on the indexing pin but align the pointers on the indexing plates visually.

This same marking technique can be used with any machine if one of the indexing points has, for whatever strange reason, more play than the others.

To verify the precision of the yoke indexing on your machine, loosen the yoke clamp, twist the yoke to the left and clamp it into place. Make a pencil mark across the joint of the two plates of the indexing assembly as indicated by the arrow in Fig. 3-78. Now release the yoke clamp and twist the yoke to the right and clamp it back into place. If there is any difference in the line-up of your pencil mark, you have play in the yoke indexing. Repeat the test with all four indexing positions.

# Precision Testing

# Rip Scales

Using the heel and toe testing jig of Procedure 9, it is quite easy to test for heeling in both rip positions.

Fig 3-79 *Testing heel and toe*

Unplug the machine, remove the blade guard and dust off the table. Put the saw into one of the rip positions. Place the heel and toe jig against the fence as shown in Fig. 3-79. Spin the blade backward with a flick of the wrist and then move the blade in toward the jig until one or more teeth just begin to scrape the end of one of the dowels on the jig. This will cause the blade to "sing". Clamp down the carriage-to-arm rip clamp and check that the blade still sings. With the blade spinning backward, slide the jig along the fence to the other end of the blade. If it sings differently, you have a heel and toe problem. Actually, this test is so precise that you can hear differences that you don't need to adjust.

Study all four possible causes listed above in the order they are listed. One of them will solve your problem.

The rip scales are not terribly precise but they are useful for getting on the right track. For precise rip cutting you should first use the scale to position the saw in the right area. Next, use a tape to the fence to get approximately right, then cut about one inch into a piece of scrap wood. Then back it out of the saw and measure the actual rip in the wood for precision. Adjust the position of the saw if necessary and test again until you have the cut you need.

Remember that the position of the rip scale indicator will change every time a blade of a different thickness is put on the machine. I don't change my indicator that often simply because I don't rely on the rip scale for precise measurement.

Whether you rely on the rip scale or not, it should be calibrated with the dynamic action of the blade and not statically with a tape measure. To set the in-rip indicator, unplug the machine, set the saw into the in-rip position, spin the saw blade backward with a flip of the wrist and slowly approach the fence until it just begins to "sing". That is 0 inches. For the out-rip, place a board at least 2″ wide between the fence and the saw in the out-rip position, spin the blade backward and approach until it "sings" against the edge of the board. Set the out-rip indicator to the exact width of the board being used.

## Craftsman

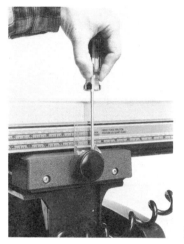

On the Craftsman, the in-rip scale is on the right side of the arm, the out-rip scale on the left side of the arm. A simple holding screw needs to be loosened, the indicator moved and the screw retightened.

Fig 3-80

## DeWalt

On the DeWalt both the rip scales are on the right side of the arm. You must set the out-rip indicator first, using the mounting screws. Then the in-rip indicator is set by simply pushing the movable indicator to the proper position.

Fig 3-81

## Rockwell

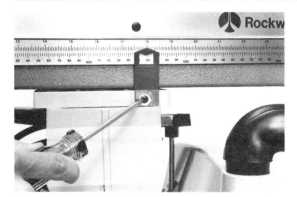

On the Rockwell, the out-rip scale is on the left of the arm and the in-rip on the right of the arm. The indicators are simply adjusted by loosening the mounting screws.

Fig 3-82

## Adjusting Splitters

Splitters are basically wedges of some kind that are wider than the saw blade but narrower than the kerf (tooth set usually makes the cut wider than the body of the blade itself). They are located behind the blade during ripping operations to prevent wood from closing in and binding on the blade. They are usually mounted together with the anti-kickback teeth.

Splitters are not absolutely essential but they make the operations safer, especially with green wood or wood that is under stress and tends to warp radically when ripped. They are also quite useful for controlling narrow pieces between the blade and the fence. On some models they also serve as a rear blade guard, covering the rear approach to the spinning blade.

**DeWalt**

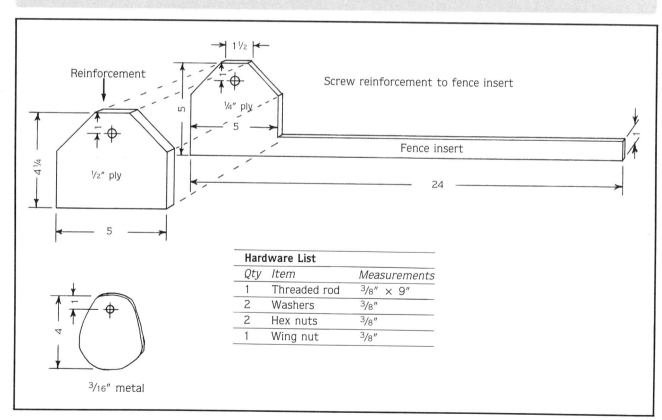

Fig 3-84 *Splitter*

## Craftsman

Fig 3-83

On the Craftsman, the splitter is a round disc mounted with the anti-kickback teeth. If you change the blade on the saw, you may have to adjust the splitter left or right to ensure that it lines up with the new cut. Leave the splitter high and rip a board for about one foot of its length. This will provide a kerf cut directly under the splitter. Turn off the saw, drop the splitter and adjust the two hex nuts that position it left to right on its mounting so that the disc centers in the kerf cut.

## DeWalt

Splitters are available with only the DeWalt industrial saws. An efficient homemade model can be built as shown in Fig. 3-84 and Fig. 3-85. It is limited to use on narrow boards, but that is when we need it most.

Fig 3-85

## Rockwell

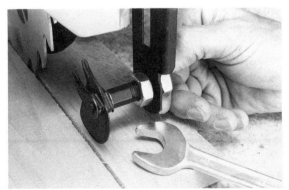

Fig 3-86

On the Rockwell, the splitter is an oval disc mounted with the anti-kickback teeth. If you change the blade on the saw you may have to adjust the splitter left or right to ensure that it lines up with the new cut. Leave the splitter high and rip a board for about one foot of its length. This will provide a kerf cut directly under the splitter. Turn off the saw, drop the splitter and adjust the two hex nuts that position it left to right on its mounting so that it fits inside the kerf cut.

## Kerf Cutting into Table

Fig 3-87 *Kerfing table*

We now have a perfectly lined up saw and a nice new clean protective cover on top of the table. You will want to cut into this new top just enough to allow you to change from cross cutting operations to in-rip or out-rip and slide from one rip dimension to another without having to crank the saw upward and then back downward.

Secure the arm-to-column clamp so that the saw will cut perfectly square from the fence. Place the saw above the table surface and turn it on. Slowly drop the saw until it just grazes the surface. Push the saw back to the rear of the arm and lower it 1/8". Now draw it all the way to the front of the arm, cutting into the table cover as you go. You need to be careful that this cut is no more than half way through the protective cover.

With the saw at the extreme front end of the arm, clamp down the carriage-to-arm lock (rip lock). With the motor still running, loosen the yoke clamp and carefully swing the saw around to the out-rip position. Lock the yoke clamp and release the rip clamp. Now gently push the saw sideways towards the fence. If it doesn't want to go, raise it a fraction of an inch and try again. It will cut on the side of the tips of the teeth, carving out a trough in the middle of the table. Push about halfway back. You can lower it and make another cut if you had raised it before.

Bring the saw back to the front, lock the rip clamp and release the yoke clamp. Swing the saw around to the in-rip position, lock the yoke clamp and release the rip clamp. Now push the saw all the way back to the fence.

Your table should now look like the one in Fig. 3-87.

Congratulations. You now have a radial arm saw that runs like a finely tuned sports car. The time invested in learning these techniques will soon pay off with greater ease and satisfaction in your woodworking. Besides, when you go to touch up the adjustments the next time, it will only take a couple of minutes.

# Chapter 4

# Quick Daily Check

At the beginning of a working day, or prior to any very important finish cuts, you may want to run a quick check on alignment. There are only three steps to this quick check.

## Check for Heel and Toe Alignment

## Check for Blade Square to Fence

Place the heel-and-toe jig in either the cross cut or rip position and test the blade for vertical heel-and-toe. See Fig. 3-56 for the jig and Chapter 3, Procedure 9 (Section 9.2) for how to use it. Adjust only if necessary.

Trim the end of a 12″ board using the technique for precision squaring to the fence explained in Chapter 3, Procedure 10 (Section 10.1). Adjust only if necessary.

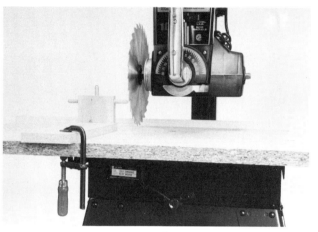

Fig 4-1 *Quick test, heel and toe*

Fig 4-2 *Quick test, square to fence*

## Check for Blade Square to Table

Place a $1'' \times 3''$ board upright against the fence and cut through, checking for the blade square to the table as explained in Chapter 3, Procedure 11 (Section 11.1). Adjust only if necessary.

The last two tests require scrap wood that is straight and has two sides parallel. It is useful to make up several of these boards and keep them aside. You will be more inclined to run the tests regularly if you don't have to stop in the middle of a project to make up a test board.

Fig 4-3 *Quick test, square to table*

# Chapter 5

# Inaccuracies Induced by Operation of the Saw

Even after the saw has been precisely lined up, it is possible to introduce inaccuracies during use. All of these problems can either be avoided or compensated for once you understand what causes them.

## Blade Lift Causing Bevel Angle Change

The blade is not located directly under the motor support yoke, but off to the left side. During cross cut operations, the blade comes from the top down into the wood and the resistance to the cut causes an upward force on the blade. Were the blade located directly under its mounting yoke, this would have no significant effect on the cut, but since it is off to the side it tends to pivot up creating a slight angle from the intended 90°. If the bevel clamp is not firmly tightened, the blade would visibly pivot up as seen in the photo below. This upward force is greater if you cut harder wood, if you move faster through the wood, or if the blade is dull.

Fig 5-1 *Blade pivot during cutting*

Even when the bevel clamp is secure, the flexibility of the entire assembly can cause a slight pivoting and hence less precision to the cut if there is sufficient upward force. There is less upward pivoting force when you cut slowly and with a sharp blade. If the wood is hard you can minimize this force by grazing the edge of the work, cutting into less wood.

The double cut technique (a rough work cut followed immediately by a delicate precision cut) will overcome the inherent flexibility of the radial arm saw.

If I need an absolutely square cut, when cutting the delicate wedges of a massive Backgammon table, for example, I will first cut through the wood normally. If my good piece is on the left, I will leave about 1/16″ of scrap because the blade will be undercutting on the left. Then I will reposition my piece and graze the edge slowly and easily with a very sharp blade and it will come out square. If my good piece is on the right, I simply cut two times without having to reposition the wood. The first pass will leave a little extra on the bottom because of the blade twisting away from the wood on the right, and the second pass will come back and remove this almost imperceptible bevel leaving the wood dead square.

## Blade Lift Causing Raised Dado Cuts

When a wide dado is cut across a wide piece of hardwood, there is a great deal of upward force. This tends to lift the arm, raising the blade out of the wood slightly. This will not only cause the dado to be less than full depth on the end of its cut, but it will cause the saw to attempt to run forward. Again, it is often a question of the sharpness of the blade and the hardness of the wood. When the roller head is as loose as most of them usually are, the dado cut can become impossible.

Under good conditions, you can usually make good dados simply by slowing down the rate of feed. Pull the saw more slowly. If your saw is properly tightened up and aligned, you will find that it already works better than ever before on this difficult cut. But despite all of that, there are occasions when it just doesn't want to work. The bite is simply too big for the weight and force of the motor. This time we will use two techniques together to solve the problem: double cutting and push cutting.

Raise the blade above the wood and then using the crank as a measuring device (see Chapter 3, Procedure 5, Section 5.5) bring it down to the wood and then into the wood at least $1/16''$ if not about half of your dado depth. Draw this across the wood. This will effortlessly score the top of the wood and prevent any splinters in the next step. In some cases you can simply drop the saw lower and make the second cut in the normal drawing-forward fashion. Under difficult conditions, you will have to make the second cut as a push cut.

A push cut involves pulling the saw to the full front end of the arm, lowering it into position or sliding the wood into position and pushing the saw back toward the column, cutting wood as you go. *Warning:* The blade is cutting on the up-stroke and although this makes the cut easier to control, it tends to lift the wood off the table and into the blade. The saw will give you no trouble in this direction, but the wood will. You must hold the wood down firmly. If there is any difficulty in doing this by hand, use one of the hold-down jigs shown in the next chapter. If you have not scored the wood in the first step above, you will find that the dado blade rips horrible splinters off the top surface of the wood.

## Rip Pivoting

When the blade is not parallel to the fence but opens out away from the fence, a piece of wood pushed through a rip cut will certainly leave the fence and follow the blade, causing a tapered and jagged cut. But this can even happen with a properly aligned machine if the wood is fed into the cut in an improper fashion.

Fig 5-3 *Two-point push stick*

Fig 5-2 *Push stick pivoting*

The above photo shows use of a very narrow push stick applied near the fence. Since the resistance of the saw blade is greatly to the left, there will be a pivoting action, particularly near the end of the cut. The wider the board, the worse the action.

The above photo shows use of a pushing board that pushes evenly on both sides of the blade. This will eliminate the pivoting action caused by the push stick itself. Such a push board, or two-point push stick, must be long enough to push the piece of wood beyond the blade on the back side before its handle comes to a stop in contact with the blade guard. The action of these sticks can be improved by incorporating hold-down notches or even pointed pins that grab the end of the board and hold it down until it is fully through the blade.

## Miter Sliding

Precision miter cuts are often difficult because of the tendency for the piece of wood to slide along the fence during the cut.

Fig 5-4 *Sandpaper fence*

The problem can be eliminated for all normal miter cuts by simply making up a special miter fence. This is no more than a regular fence faced with 100 grit sandpaper (avoid cutting through the fence too often, as it is not good for the saw blades). Slight finger pressure will bind most woods to the fence and resist the sliding tendency.

Fig 5-5 *Miter end block*

For more precision in the cut or for repeated cuts, you will want to take the time to install an end block on the fence. This can simply be a block of wood clamped to the fence or a small home-made wooden clamp specially made for the purpose (see Chapter 6, "end stops"). The block must be used on the "open" side of the miter cut as shown in the photo above. This way the wood is always free to move away from the blade; no binding, no kicking. If the block were put on the closed-in side of the miter cut, it could be dangerous putting your fingers on that side to hold the wood tightly against the table, leaving the wood to move into the blade and bind. Also, in the open position it automatically resists the sliding tendency of the miter cut, guaranteeing you a perfect cut every time.

# Chapter 6

# Accessories Related to Precision

Many people buy radial arm saws because they are impressed with all the gadgets that they can get to work on the machine. Generally, the fancy gadgets don't impress me. There are, however, a whole series of accessories, commercial and home made, which are often overlooked but essential because they relate to precision or safety (not just safety for you, but for the saw too).

## Portability

It is difficult to transport a radial arm saw while attached to its base because it is tall and top heavy.

Fig 6-1 *Portable stand*

Although not all models lend themselves to separating the legs from the saw, with a little ingenuity it can be done. In the photo above I attached a piece of plywood to the legs in place of the table. Then the two can be quickly joined by a couple of C clamps. This way, it can easily go into the back of something as small as a station wagon. Separating the two also makes it possible for one person to transport the saw.

Whenever you transport a radial arm saw, you should arrange to remove the weight from the arm and disengage the arm-to-column pin. If you leave the pin engaged, a shift of the cargo could cause such a shock on the pin that it could break off the stops that are on the column – and that's an expensive bit of damage. Also, if the heavy motor is hanging on the arm and you hit a bump in the road, the vertical shock could bend something, probably in the column-to-table mounting.

Fig 6-2 *Transportation position*

The arm should be swung over to about 20° and clamped to the column. This disengages the pin. If there is a shock great enough to shift the arm it will move slightly against its clamp but nothing will break. Pull the motor out almost to the end of the arm and turn the motor on its side. Drop the arm until the blade guard rests firmly on the table (don't force it down). This will give the arm support at the column and at the motor in such a way that normal transportation bumping will not knock anything out of line.

## Table Extensions

With any saw, it is useful to extend the table. On the radial arm saw, left and right table wings serve for both cross cutting and ripping. If a table extension is to be permanently attached to the saw, it must support its own weight. If you leave a board hanging on the end of the saw table for a long period of time, it will create a bow in the table and throw the saw out of alignment. Having a counter next to the saw on the right and the left is an excellent arrangement. You can store things both under and over the counter, leaving just a one foot space for sliding wood on the counter top. That is much more economical than the space requirements of table saw extensions.

Fig 6-3 *Portable wings*

The photos and the graphic above show a very useful way to have a pair of portable wings that adjust quickly to any uneven terrain. The right and left sides are identical, and can be used on either side of the saw or ganged together to form one eight-foot table on a single side. If you are going to leave them attached for any period of time, you must add a support at the point where they attach to the saw table – perhaps just a 1″ × 3″ to the leg frame.

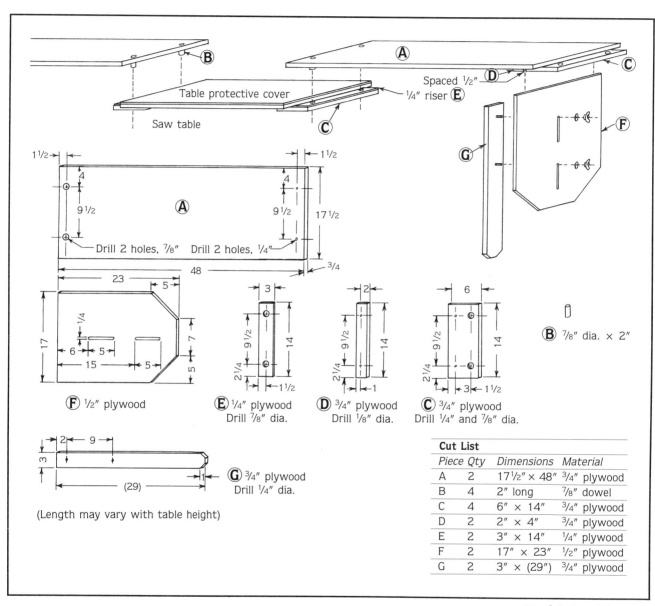

Table protective cover

Saw table

Spaced ½"

¼" riser **E**

**A**

**B**

**C**

**D**

**E**

**F**

**G**

1½  4  9½  Drill 2 holes, ⅞"  Drill 2 holes, ¼"  9½  4  1½  17½  48  ¾

23  5  ¼  17  6  5  15  5  7  5

**F** ½" plywood

3  9½  2¼  14  1½

**E** ¼" plywood
Drill ⅞" dia.

2  9½  2¼  14  1

**D** ¾" plywood
Drill ⅛" dia.

6  9½  2¼  14  3  1½

**C** ¾" plywood
Drill ¼" and ⅞" dia.

**B** ⅞" dia. × 2"

2  9  3  1  (29)

**G** ¾" plywood
Drill ¼" dia.

(Length may vary with table height)

**Cut List**

| Piece | Qty | Dimensions | Material |
|-------|-----|------------|----------|
| A | 2 | 17½" × 48" | ¾" plywood |
| B | 4 | 2" long | ⅞" dowel |
| C | 4 | 6" × 14" | ¾" plywood |
| D | 2 | 2" × 4" | ¾" plywood |
| E | 2 | 3" × 14" | ¼" plywood |
| F | 2 | 17" × 23" | ½" plywood |
| G | 2 | 3" × (29") | ¾" plywood |

Fig 6-4 *Portable wings*

## Hold-Downs and Rip Guides (Commercial)

Ripping and shaping, particularly of narrow pieces, are greatly aided by hold-downs and guides. Not only is the work faster and safer but it makes for more precise cuts as well.

Fig 6-5 *Finger hold-downs*

Fig 6-6 *Rip strate*

Spring steel fingers which can be set up on both sides of the blade are inexpensive and easy to install. They push the wood down to the table and into the fence. You can set them quite close to the blade and even alongside the blade. They can also be set too close and a saw blade is no match for their spring steel. If you adjust them too tightly against the wood, you will spend more energy pushing against the fingers than against the cut. They should be attached to their own fence insert to speed up installation. They are probably one of the best guides available for shaping as they can firmly hold narrow pieces of wood in both the horizontal and vertical directions.

The Rip Strate is a pair of spring-loaded wheels. These are mounted at a slight inward angle to the fence so that as wood is slid under they tend to push it against the fence as well as down to the table. They have a functional anti-kick-back device on the rear wheel. If you are cutting over 3″ wide you can place the wheels beside the saw blade, which gives you control for those last few inches that would otherwise have no downward pressure. Narrower cuts require the wheels to be in front of the cut. It is attached to its own fence insert, so it is very rapid to install and remove. Although considerably more expensive than the spring steel fingers, it is quicker and easier to adjust for ordinary ripping operations.

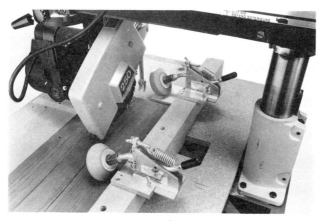

Fig 6-7 *Shophelper safety guides*

Feather boards are basically home-made versions of the spring steel fingers. They are usually made out of any springy wood from fir to maple to oak.

Cut a board to the curves desired with a jig saw. Then rip the slots to create the fingers. Test different thicknesses of fingers for different degrees of springiness. Glue 100 grit sandpaper to both sides of the part that was not ripped. This will both raise the fingers off the table so they will be free to move, and provide an easy one-clamp attachment to the table. Keep one of the boards right next to the saw along with a couple of push sticks for the emergencies you failed to anticipate.

The Shophelper Safety Guides are the most expensive of the three, but they function impressively well. They have two independent soft rubber roller wheels. Both wheels have a ratchet anti-kick-back mechanism. The forward wheel is set on the outside of the blade, while the beveled outfeed wheel is set on the fence side of the blade. They are slightly angled to the fence which pushes the wood into the fence while pushing down. There is a catch, though, in that the standard set can only be used in the in-rip position as in the photo because of the ratchet mechanisms. However, most right handers prefer to rip in this position. To use them in the out-rip position, you must dismantle and reverse the larger wheel and then buy a special orange reverse rotation beveled wheel.

The small diameter on the rear wheel makes it difficult to get it to ride up on the front edge of the board being ripped, causing a block right after starting your cut. This is easily overcome by adding a little block of scrap the thickness of the board being ripped right under this wheel to hold it up. The board will push the block out and the wheel will easily ride across from one to the other. The Shophelper should also be set up on its own fence insert for rapid installation. It has the added advantage that the wheels are installed in quick-release brackets allowing you to leave the fence in place, remove the wheels, and use the saw for cross cutting without having to change the fence.

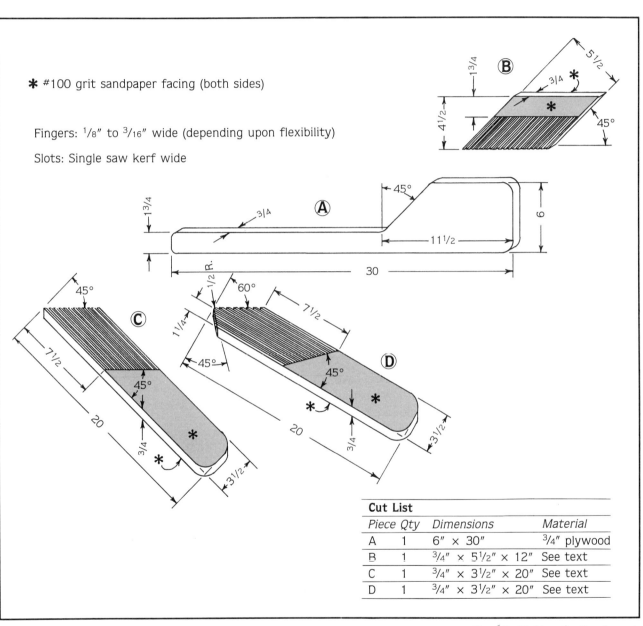

✳ #100 grit sandpaper facing (both sides)

Fingers: 1/8″ to 3/16″ wide (depending upon flexibility)

Slots: Single saw kerf wide

| Cut List | | | |
|---|---|---|---|
| Piece | Qty | Dimensions | Material |
| A | 1 | 6″ × 30″ | 3/4″ plywood |
| B | 1 | 3/4″ × 5 1/2″ × 12″ | See text |
| C | 1 | 3/4″ × 3 1/2″ × 20″ | See text |
| D | 1 | 3/4″ × 3 1/2″ × 20″ | See text |

Fig 6-8 *Making feather boards*

95

Fig 6-9 *Feather boards*

The photos show various feather boards in use. I have finally understood why all the books constantly show ripping in the out-rip position while I almost always rip in the in-rip position. The photographer complains that the motor blocks his shot. So in deference to my photographer, I even moved the motor out of the way for the second shot. Flip the feather boards over and they work just as well in the other direction.

## Raised Rip Table

The drag of the teeth in a rip cut is greatly reduced if the blade can extend beyond the wood about $^3/_4''$. On a table saw the blade is usually raised for ripping. On a radial arm saw we can obtain the same increase in ripping power by raising the wood up off the table with what I call a "raised rip table".

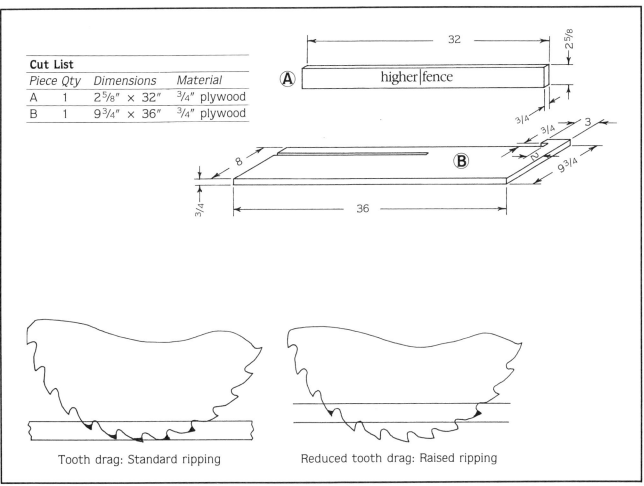

| Cut List | | | |
|---|---|---|---|
| Piece | Qty | Dimensions | Material |
| A | 1 | $2^5/_8'' \times 32''$ | $^3/_4''$ plywood |
| B | 1 | $9^3/_4'' \times 36''$ | $^3/_4''$ plywood |

Tooth drag: Standard ripping

Reduced tooth drag: Raised ripping

Fig 6-10 *Raised rip table*

Install a fence that is at least $^3/_4''$ higher than normal, or even a high one that can hold a feather board vertically. Set the saw to the proper rip width and then run the raised rip table into the blade and assure that the blade turns freely in the slot. The table lifter needs to hook on the fence or the table so that it will not advance while ripping. After a while your raised rip table will begin to look like the feather boards, but it will still hold wood up for a long time. Now you can rip in a normal fashion, but you will find that your saw has almost double the effective power.

## Push Sticks

Fig 6-11  *Push sticks*

Push sticks are made in an infinite variety of sizes, shapes and qualities ranging from simple scraps of wood to works of art.

Push sticks will either push at one point, or straddle the blade to push evenly on both sides, thereby avoiding tapered cuts. They will usually grip the wood somehow to help push it down, especially as the wood goes into the last inch of cut and moves out from under most of the hold-down devices.

You will find that the very thin lip of the push stick B in the graphic is quite useful as it will usually be able to slip under the guard, whereas the small one in the photo above can easily get blocked at the guard. The wide ''straddle'' push stick has a finishing nail with the head cut off, pointed and placed off-center. If the blade is going to hit the nail, flip the stick over and the blade will miss. This nail can be pushed into the end grain of the wood being cut. It effectively holds the wood down to the table right to the other side of the blade, but leaves the top surface free to slide completely under the guard. Always make your push sticks long enough to be able to easily reach beyond the back side of the blade, and incorporate some notch or handle that allows you to pull it back out.

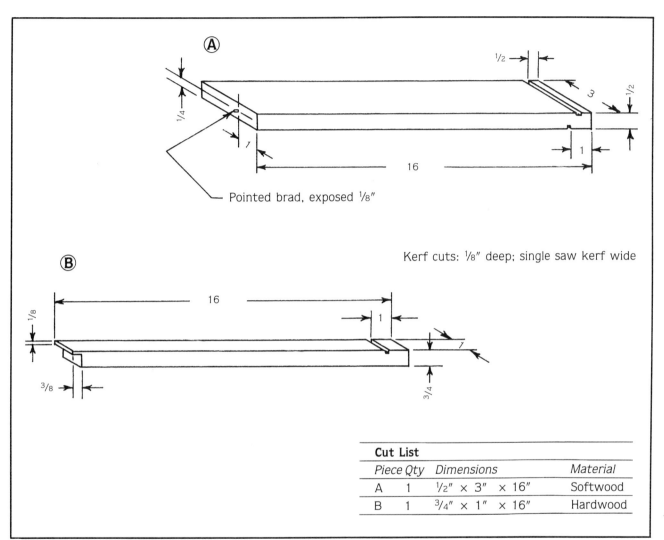

Ⓐ

¹⁄₂

³

¹⁄₄

¹⁄₂

1

16

1

Pointed brad, exposed ¹⁄₈"

Kerf cuts: ¹⁄₈" deep; single saw kerf wide

Ⓑ

16

¹⁄₈

1

⁷

³⁄₈

³⁄₄

| Cut List | | | |
|---|---|---|---|
| Piece | Qty | Dimensions | Material |
| A | 1 | ¹⁄₂" × 3" × 16" | Softwood |
| B | 1 | ³⁄₄" × 1" × 16" | Hardwood |

Fig 6-12 *Push sticks*

**99**

## Splinter Back-Up

When cross cutting, the saw blade enters the wood on the top and the front faces. It leaves the wood on the table and the fence sides and if there is not proper support on these two sides, the blade will break surface splinters away as it comes through the wood. For an especially important cut, I will shift my fence an inch or two to the right or left and then make a fresh cut through it. This tells me exactly where my blade will come through, allowing me to mark my wood and line it up to the fence slot with precision (for this purpose I always make my fences at least 1/4″ higher than my work). In addition, it provides a complete back-up against splinters. To stop splinters on the bottom side of the work, I throw a fresh piece of Masonite onto the table, place my piece and cut through. The fresh cut in the Masonite will exactly match the blade width, leaving solid splinter support on both sides of the cut.

The strap hinge on the first jig hooks around the fence and bends under the table so that the hold down pressure will not pop the fence out of the table. The adjustable pad allows for pressure at the right spot. This particular jig is a bit of trouble to install and I only use it when I need it. The other hold-down hooks over the front edge of the table. The curve keeps your fingers away from the blade, while the pad can be angled in right next to the blade. The second does not give as much pressure as the first, but it is easy to grab and put to use even after the beginning of a cut.

Fig 6-13 *Fence hold-down jig*

The last guarantee against unwanted splinters is to assure that the wood is held tightly against the clean table top. To do this, I use one of several hold-down devices that all serve to push the wood hard to the table. They are also extremely useful for holding tiny pieces that would draw your fingers too close to the blade.

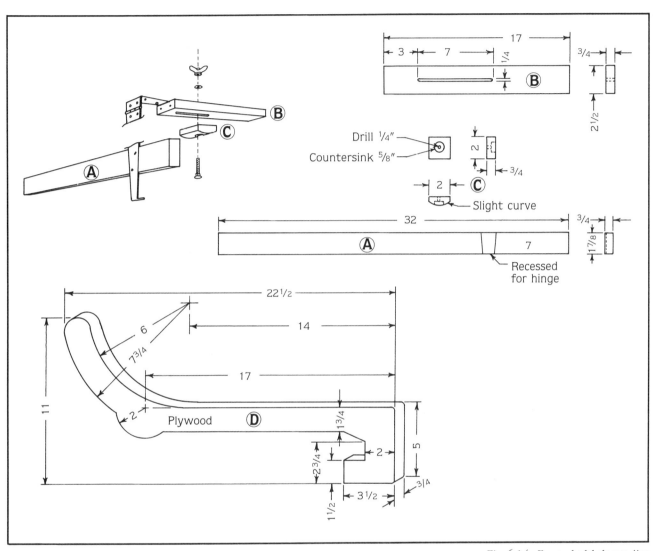

17

3  7  1/4  B  3/4

2 1/2

Drill 1/4"
Countersink 5/8"

2

3/4

2  C

Slight curve

32  3/4

A  7  1 7/8

Recessed
for hinge

22 1/2

6  14

7 3/4

17

11  2

Plywood  D  1 3/4

2 3/4  2  5

1 1/2  3 1/2  3/4

Fig 6-14 *Fence hold-down jigs*

## End Stops

End stops attached to the fence can be very useful. They can be as simple as a scrap of wood clamped to the fence or as fancy as the lever clamp below. The lever clamp's main advantage is that you don't have to try to turn a clamp handle where there is no space to do so. Whatever you use, there are several important considerations for both precision and security.

Fig 6-15 *End stops*

If the wood is to be tight between the clamp and the saw blade, you must keep your hand on that part of the wood. It has no freedom to move so it must not move or it will kick. This is generally easy to hold on to on the left side of the saw, so my lever clamp has no special provisions for that side. The right side, however, is very hard to grip because of the motor. Because of this, there is a movable spacer on the end stop which allows placing the board at the right distance from the blade, raising the spacer to free the board on that end and allowing safe cutting. The lever clamp has sandpaper facing on the surfaces that grip the fence. This keeps it from moving without undue clamping pressure.

You will also want to make sure that your end stop does not quite reach the table top. This will allow sawdust to slide under it and away. Otherwise, the dust will collect against the spacer and your boards will become shorter and shorter.

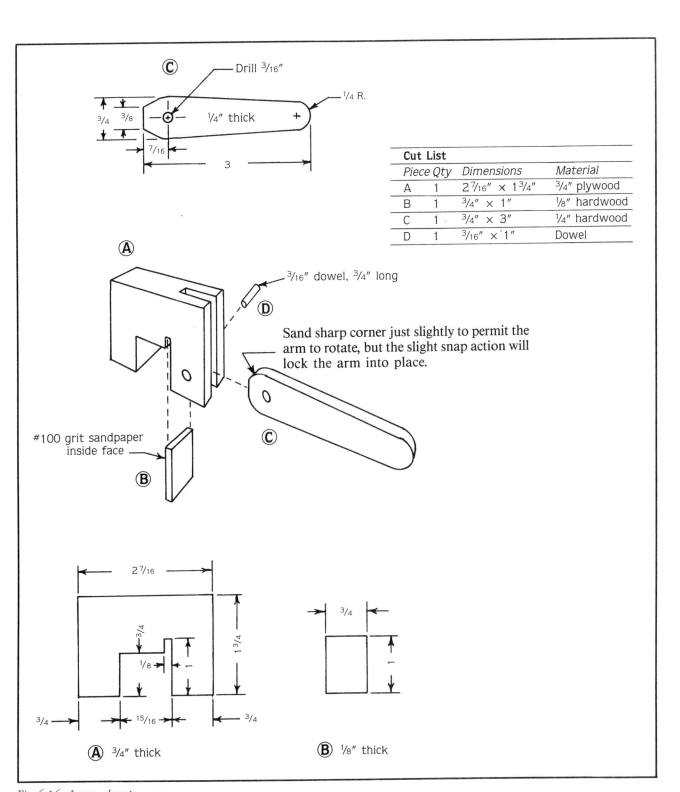

©     — Drill ³/₁₆″

¹/₄ R.

³/₄   ³/₈    ¹/₄″ thick    +

⁷/₁₆

3

**Cut List**

| Piece | Qty | Dimensions | Material |
|-------|-----|------------|----------|
| A | 1 | 2⁷/₁₆″ × 1³/₄″ | ³/₄″ plywood |
| B | 1 | ³/₄″ × 1″ | ¹/₈″ hardwood |
| C | 1 | ³/₄″ × 3″ | ¹/₄″ hardwood |
| D | 1 | ³/₁₆″ ×'1″ | Dowel |

Ⓐ

³/₁₆″ dowel, ³/₄″ long

Ⓓ

Sand sharp corner just slightly to permit the arm to rotate, but the slight snap action will lock the arm into place.

#100 grit sandpaper inside face

Ⓒ

Ⓑ

2⁷/₁₆

³/₄

¹/₈

1³/₄

1

³/₄    ¹⁵/₁₆    ³/₄

Ⓐ ³/₄″ thick

³/₄

1

Ⓑ ¹/₈″ thick

Fig 6-16 *Lever clamp*

103

## Specialty Fences

You should have the message by now that it is a good idea to have several fences, all ready to use at the appropriate time. They are not expensive and the right fence at the right time or a new fence to allow a fresh identifiable cross cut saves time and gives precision.

Gluing 100 grit sandpaper to the fence will convert the fence into a slip-proof miter fence. You should have a high fence to hold a vertical feather board, a medium fence to go beyond a raised rip table, special open fences for shaping, perhaps a smooth fence with no notches for ripping, and fences which hold your spring steel fingers, roller guides or hold-down clamps. You can have offset fences to move the fence in away from the column for some horizontal saw cutting. But above all you need a number of ordinary sized, very straight fences to allow you to change them often, keeping the fence relatively clean and always giving you the ability to make a completely fresh cut backed up against splinters.

## Electricity

Many saws have the option of working at 110 or 220 volts. In fact, if the full amperage is available at the saw in a 110 volt installation, there is no real advantage to the 220-volt installation. It is commonly believed that operating at 220 volts is inherently better. This belief apparently stems from the fact that when installed at 220 volts, the saw usually has its own special properly-sized power supply. When operated at 110 volts, it is often on the end of a 100-foot run and sharing the power with light bulbs, washing machines and who knows what else.

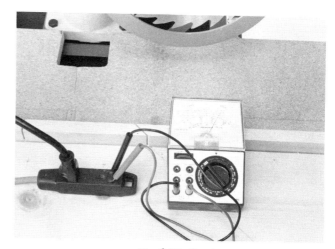

Fig 6-17 *Testing delivered voltage*

If your saw is running on 110 volts and seems to lack power, try simply plugging a volt meter into the same outlet that the saw is plugged into. While the saw is off, you will certainly read the full 117 volts. Now turn on the saw and watch the voltmeter. If the line is too long, too small or sharing with too many other things, you will hear that your saw is having trouble getting started and you will see the voltage indicator drop radically. Once the motor is running, it should come back up close to the no-load voltage. If it doesn't, you really have a problem. Now give the saw something solid to cut and watch the volt meter. If the meter drops to 90 volts under heavy load you may very well burn out your motor. The problem is that there is simply not enough amperage coming through the line, hence the voltage drops as well. Either give the saw its own 12-gauge power line as short as possible from the distribution panel, or give it its own 220 volt line. Most burnt-out motors are caused by a combination of dull blades (they require more electricity) and long extension cords.

Fig 6-18 *Lower blade guards*

The lower blade guards on these saws are generally flimsy. I have seen industrial efforts to make better ones, but I have yet to see any lower blade guards that make any sense for anything other than a straight forward 90° cross cut or an uncomplicated rip cut. As soon as you go over something (sometimes even just the fence) or turn on the slightest angle (without mentioning horizontal work), the lower blade guards become more of a menace than a protection. In fact, the manufacturers know this and when they can get away with it, they don't even include them in the package. In every shop that I have ever seen, they are removed and lost.

To work properly, the inside one would have to be attached to the motor housing, not to the blade guard. This would eliminate the problem that they are generally a major obstruction to changing the blade. They would have to move up easily when encountering any shape or thickness of wood and not bind when on a bevel angle. They would have to be very lightly spring-loaded so that they could continue to function in the horizontal position. I have yet to find a set of lower blade guards that are more useful than troublesome. When I have a radial that is serving a straight cut-off function and being used by a lot of different people (e.g., on a construction site), I install the lower blade guards.

The arm that comes down from the blade guard with the anti-kick-back fingers is another story. Its anti-kick-back function is valuable, but more importantly it serves as a rear end stop that prevents the wood from rising up significantly. It also becomes a rigid cover for the back of the blade, one that will not move out of the way like the lower blade guards. This is important when you are reaching around your saw to receive wood on the back side of a rip cut – there is something solid between you and the blade. Always adjust it properly for rip cuts (it only takes 5 seconds). Many people even lower it for cross cutting, providing a solid obstruction in front of the advancing blade.

The greatest safety combination of all is a sharp blade, a precisely lined up saw and a patient woodworker.